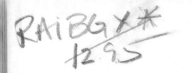

Beyond Generation X

A Practical Guide for Managers

by Claire Raines

CRISP PUBLICATIONS
MENLO PARK, CA

Beyond Generation X

A Practical Guide for Managers

by Claire Raines

M 3 781 5 757

CREDITS

Managing Editor: Kathleen Barcos
Editor: Follin Armfield
Production: Leslie Power
Typesetting: ExecuStaff
Cover Design: 5th Street Design

Copyright © 1997 by Crisp Publications, Inc.
Printed in the United States of America by Bawden Printing Company.

Distribution to the U.S. Trade:

National Book Network, Inc.
4720 Boston Way
Lanham, MD 20706
1-800-462-6420

Library of Congress Catalog Card Number 97-65866
Raines, Claire
Beyond Generation X
ISBN 1-56052-449-9

CONTENTS

ACKNOWLEDGMENTS

*I*n many ways, this book is like a patchwork quilt: the best pieces were given by friends. Thank you, thank you, thank you to:

✗ Terry Murphy, Karen Tracy, and everybody at Wendy's International. You made me part of the Wendy's family.

✗ Judy Shannon of Hyatt Regency Hotels. I have been inspired to watch you take the *Twentysomething* information and cause grass-roots change!

✗ AlphaGraphics owners and managers: Tammy, Bill, and Carolyn Bradish, Store #116 in Littleton, Colorado; Carl Cooper, Store #369 in Nogales, Arizona; Rick and Dianne Ernst, Store #120 in Concord, California.

✗ Tami Kaiser from Promus Hotels.

✗ Kathy Watkins from Fazoli's Italian Food Restaurants.

✗ Patrick Gammon of Sodexho.

✗ Jana Springer and Lee Cockerell from Walt Disney World.

✗ Karen O'Brien Butterworth from Kingston Plantation.

✗ Josie Peterson from Richfield Hospitality Services.

✗ Sean Conley from Marie Callendar's.

✗ Ed Howie and Rob Taylor from Chick-fil-A.

✗ Arleen Arnsparger at the Education Commission of the States. Your knowledge and insights about the school system were invaluable to me.

✗ Friends and colleagues Linda Williamson and Marjorie Allison. Your creative additions added delight to the process.

✗ Jim Hunt. Thank you, dear friend, fellow author, and editor extraordinaire for scrutinizing every phrase and making suggestions that not only made sense but a world of difference.

IT'S A BUSINESS ISSUE

$\mathcal{E}$mployers in the service industries have moved employee retention to the top of the list of cost-containment measures. It has become the bottom-line criterion for staying in business. Not only are companies confronting the high expense of replacing employees, they are finding it increasingly difficult to locate new recruits.

The *Wall Street Journal* estimates it costs somewhere between $2,900 and $10,000 to replace a "shift-ready" manager. In Houston, Larry Forehand, president of the Texas Restaurant Association, sat down to figure some of his company's most expensive labor costs. Here is what he found to be average replacement costs for four positions at Casa Olé:

Kitchen Employee	$775
Host	$658
Server	$474
Busser	$362

What he discovered next is startling: if a restaurant has to replace one person per month in each category—and, in an industry with turnover rates somewhere above 200%, that's altogether possible—it would cost the business nearly **$30,000 annually**. That's why employers say the "labor crunch" is their top concern.

This book offers solutions to the growing labor crisis. It is a compact, useful, and practical manual for busy, perhaps frustrated, managers.

If you are managing employees in their teens and twenties, this book was written for you. It will give you a brief overview of members of Generation X—who they are, how they're different, and why. To make sure you get practical, down-to-earth information—not theory—each section includes the reactions of a Generation X worker. Most important, the book offers you a 188-item "laundry list" of tools, tips, and techniques—creative ideas you can implement immediately.

I hope you find lots of insights here. But what I really hope is that you will become a better manager by using these ideas to recruit, manage, motivate, and retain the best and brightest of today's new workforce!

Claire Raines
Denver, Colorado
January, 1997

ABOUT THE NAMES WE CALL PEOPLE

*T*he generation born after the Baby Boom has been given many labels: Post-Boomers, Baby Busters, Slackers, Twentysomethings, Generation X, The Thirteenth Generation.

In this book, two terms—*Twentysomethings* and *Generation X*—are used to speak of the same group of people. *Twentysomething* is a neutral, descriptive term that simply defines the ages—late teens and twenties—of today's new generation of workers. *Generation X* is a term first coined by Canadian novelist Douglas Coupland to describe his own generation—a generation he feels defies labels.

PART ONE

THE NEED FOR A BRIDGE

The Top 10 Things Managers Do That Drive Their Younger Employees Crazy

(or, 10 Sure-Fire Ways to Increase Turnover)

10. Give raises that are virtually meaningless (a few cents an hour).

9. Give insincere, gratuitous "thank yous" and pats on the back.

8. Throw people into jobs they're not trained for or qualified to do.

7. Allow the workplace to be disorganized, cluttered, or dirty.

6. Share the stress of a visit from a district or corporate visitor with the whole staff.

5. Answer questions with, "Because I said so"—or an answer that reflects that attitude.

4. Overlook unacceptable behavior from staff members.

3. Ignore employee opinions and ideas.

2. Fail to give feedback and regular performance reviews.

1. Micromanage.

CHAPTER ONE

ARE YOU THE MANAGER?

*I*f you're reading this book to understand your twentysomething employees better, chances are you're a manager in your thirties or forties. If so, you are a member of the Baby Boom generation, born between 1946 and 1964. You are a member of the biggest, most powerful, most influential generation in modern times.

Managers, supervisors, crew leaders, foremen in thirties and forties

Chances are you have worked very, very hard to get where you are today. You paid your dues. Likely, you have put in many weekends and evenings over the years to build your career. You care deeply about the quality of your work, and much of your personal identity is tied up in the job you do. Over the years, you have struggled with your share of difficult bosses, unreasonable policies, and tough situations. Sometimes you found ways to live with them; other times, you found solutions elsewhere. But, always, you have stayed committed to doing a good job—a really good job, whatever you were doing.

Hard workers

Somewhat puzzled by today's younger employees

If you're typical of your generation of managers, you're somewhat baffled—perhaps even frustrated—by the new breed of young workers. Your colleagues tell me they just don't understand their younger employees. They complain that their Gen X employees aren't committed and have no work ethic. They question their loyalty. They tell me that if their younger employees are scheduled to get off at 5:00 P.M., they're gone at 5:01 P.M.—even if the work group is in the midst of an important project. They say they're tired of hearing young workers ask, "What's in it for me?"

If even part of this is true for you, hang in there. I think I can help. For the past five years, I've worked extensively with managers and their Generation X employees in a variety of industries. Yes, today's new workforce is *different* from yesterday's. They grew up in a very different world, and they hold a different view of work. But they make outstanding employees—if *we* are willing to take a little time to understand them and adapt our management styles and work environment to meet their unique needs.

We're Not Asking Too Much
by Michael Cotton

I have heard many Baby Boomers complain they just do not understand our generation. The problem is they do not *try* to understand us. Because they belong to the largest generation in history, they believe every other generation must follow their lead. They expect us to have the same work ethic, devotion, and loyalty.

We have no desire to follow their lead. We are a unique generation with our own set of values. Our personal experiences and the world we grew up in helped shape these values. We want to make our mark on the world—and we want to do it on our own terms.

Don't get me wrong. Most of us admire and respect the Baby Boomers' work ethic. They paid a high price, though. Work became their lives and the key to their personal identities. We have seen the toll it took on other parts of their lives. Just look at the Boomers' divorce rate. We do not want to pay that price. We are more than willing to work hard and pay our dues, but work is only a part of life, not the whole thing. We refuse to sacrifice the important things in life for the sake of work, and we do not want our personal identities tied to our jobs.

We have seen that hard work and loyalty do not always lead to the expected rewards. We grew up in the 1980s. We were led to believe that hard work and loyalty would be rewarded with a good job and secure future.

When it came our turn to join the "real world," however, the entire landscape shifted. The promise of job security disappeared almost overnight.

We learned that loyalty is not a two-way street as we saw middle managers laid off after years of service.

Many Baby Boomers complain that we are a bunch of whiners who are unwilling to pay our dues. The Baby Boomers fail to realize that our circumstances are truly different. Most of us graduate from college with heavy debt loads—and all we can find are menial jobs.

Contrary to the stereotype, we do not expect to start out at the top. However, we do expect a job that is somewhat interesting—and pays a decent salary that will help us pay off our debts, establish our lives, and at least make our college education seem worthwhile.

We do not feel this is asking too much.

Michael P. Cotton, 25, holds an MBA in international business. He is an accountant.

"In our office, we have typewriters and we have computers. The boomers will choose the typewriter or a pad of paper every time. It drives me nuts!"

—Jennet Hunt, Graduate Student, Age 26

X

Top Attributes of Generation X Employees

1. *They are good at change.*
   As children of divorced parents, many learned to adapt to a new bedroom, different home, and new neighborhood on weekends and holidays.

2. *They are comfortable with technology.*
   They know how to set the clock on the VCR!

3. *They are independent.*
   Many took on adult responsibilities and learned to take care of themselves at an early age.

4. *They are financially savvy.*
   They know how far a dollar goes.

5. *They are not intimidated by authority.*
   They don't seek approval from those in charge.

6. *They are creative.*
   They add a fresh perspective to problem-solving and strategy sessions.

CHAPTER TWO

WHO IS GENERATION X?

Born 1960–1980

Workers in their teens and twenties

The primary labor supply for the next 10 years

An endangered species

Generation X grew up in the shadow of the Baby Boom, which demographers traditionally have defined as those born between 1946 and 1964. Generation X's first official birth year, then, was 1965, the year the birthrate dropped below 4 million. For the 11 previous years, the United States had consistently produced more than 4 million new babies each year; after 1964, it would be an astounding 25 years before that number would be reached again.

To define Generation X, it's necessary first to clarify them in relation to the Baby Boom—a fact most Xers are all too aware of. The Baby Boomers grew up in the spotlight. New products—from slinkies to pre-teen-sized clothing—were created especially for them. Schools, subdivisions, and shopping malls expanded to make room for them. Never in history had a generation been so pampered, so idealized, so focused on. For 50 years, they have taken center stage.

Then along came Generation X, a bit like the younger sibling following behind the older sister—the older sister who just

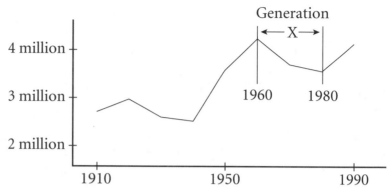

Yearly U.S. Birthrate
in Millions

Generation
←—X—→

4 million

3 million   1960   1980

2 million

1910   1950   1990

(Source: U.S. National Center for Health Statistics)

happened to have been homecoming queen, cheerleader, National
Honor Society member, and class president. Then she took her
place in the workforce, where she continued to put everything
she had into whatever she did. Today, she and her cohorts are
ensconced in the desirable jobs. As one young woman said,
"The Baby Boom took so much and left us so dry."

Though Generation X demographically begins with birth year
1965, most people born in the early sixties will tell you they
identify more with the Generation X personality than with the
Baby Boom. For that reason, when we look at manager-employer
issues, we are probably best served by thinking of Generation X
as those born from 1960 to 1980. They are our employees who
are in their teens and twenties and even early thirties today.

This group of people will provide our primary supply of new
labor for the next 10 years, and, as we have already noted, they
are an endangered species—at least in the service industries.
Suffering from the shrinking labor pool, hotels, restaurants, and
stores are facing the effects of two-thirds of a million fewer new
workers per year.

This new generation is known by a variety of labels. They were first called the Post-Boomers or the Baby-Bust Generation. In 1991, in their book *Generations: The History of America's Future, 1584 to 2069* (William Morrow), William Strauss and Neil Howe called them "Thirteeners" since they were the thirteenth generation of Americans born since the Declaration of Independence. When Larry Bradford and I wrote our book* we called them "Twentysomethings," a fairly neutral term that was popular in the press at the time. At about the same time, a young novelist, Douglas Coupland, himself a member of this generation, wrote a novel about some of his cohorts. He announced that he didn't like any of the titles his generation had been given. For one thing, the names were being handed out by Baby Boomers, the generation he found self-righteous and critical of his generation. He also pointed out that this new generation of young people defies labels. "Just call us Generation Xs,'" he implored.

Coupland's caution about labels is worth noting. Labels can be very dangerous. They can lead to stereotyping. They can be self-fulfilling (look at what happens in the schools when we smack a label on a child). They can oversimplify people, allowing folks to categorize others rather than really getting to know them as individuals.

And yet, it is nearly impossible to learn about something until we name it. Once we have a label, we can differentiate it, see what's unique about it, study its origins, and begin to develop a clearer understanding of it. We can slow down and study the mechanism and our responses to it, so that when the machine starts back up and is in the midst of real-time, dynamic events and relationships, we can incorporate what we've learned into our ongoing behaviors.

As we travel together, exploring this group of people we call Generation X, let us label with care. Let us remember the dangers and be cautious about them, while fully realizing the benefits.

Twentysomething: Managing and Motivating Today's New Work Force. Alexander-Merrill Publishing, 1992.

From an Xpert

Labels and Stereotypes
BY KEN MARZORATI

If I were required to choose one label for my generation, it would be "Gen E." for "entitlements, please." We demand the same quality of life, standard of living, big houses, big cars, and big money as the Boomers had—simply because, well, they had it. Why can't we? But the world changes, and so should we. The Boomers didn't get what they've got by saying, "I want, I want, I want." They went out and did something to get it.

Stereotypes about my generation get in the way. A few years back, I had an eight-hour interview with a technical services provider. I arrived in a black blazer and jeans, with my shoulder-length red hair tied back. The receptionist asked if I was lost. I told her I had an interview, but she didn't believe me and demanded a photo ID. The first few staff members I met looked me over, asked a few conciliatory questions, and dismissed me to the next manager on the list. Only after I was able to resolve a technical problem their engineers had been struggling with, was I taken seriously.

If both sides—Boomers and Xers alike—could set down their labels, the working world would be a better place.

Ken Marzorati, 30, is a technical consultant. He has held jobs as telephone designer, communications analyst, call center manager, researcher, and technical writer. Ken lives in Michigan.

"I don't look at chaos and think it's bad. I walk with it—not through it."

—Jennet Hunt, Graduate Student, Age 26

Managers' Most Common Complaints About Twentysomething Employees

"I call them Generation Y—they ask *why* about every assignment."

"They're not willing to pay their dues."

"They are materialistic. They think they have to have a CD player, cappuccino maker, computer, and all the things that go with them."

"They're not willing to 'go the extra mile.' If their shift ends at 5:00 and we're in the middle of a project, they're outta here."

"They're cynical. They have a dim view of the world and what's going on."

"They don't show up. And they don't even call to tell me why."

"They're not committed—to me, the job, or the company."

"They have no respect for authority. They'll waltz right in and sit at the head of the conference room table."

"They're far more interested in things other than their jobs."

"They want things *now.*"

CHAPTER THREE

WHY WORRY?

A critical, bottom-line business issue

Shrinking labor pool

Clashing work ethics

Business results tied to frontline

*E*ffective management of young employees is not just "the right thing to do" anymore. Today it is a critical business issue. America's primary labor supply for the next decade represents the smallest population group in U.S. history and the shallowest pool of entry-level workers in modern times. There simply are not enough of them to go around, particularly in the service industries. For almost a decade, some business owners have turned a skeptical eye on the reality of the shrinking labor pool. In the last couple of years, most have become true believers.

Take a walk through a nearby shopping mall: you will find that every door has a "Help Wanted" sign. Ski area officials in Vail, Colorado, estimate that last winter nearly 2000 jobs went unfilled because there weren't enough applicants in town. It got so bad the local McDonald's closed in the afternoon because there weren't enough warm bodies to staff it. Executives at the corporate head-quarters of Wendy's International in Dublin, Ohio, have been pulled in to work the lunch hour at the Wendy's down the street.

The problem becomes particularly complex when managers and employees clash over work-ethic issues. Turnover is typically 200% in restaurants and hotels, and some experts estimate it costs as much as $600 to replace one lost worker. The cost of attracting, hiring, and training replacements cuts deeply into the profit margin.

Business results depend on front-line workers, on how they interact with your customers, handle merchandise, understand your product. To thrive—even survive—businesses must meet the challenges of managing this new generation of workers head-on.

Las Vegas' Shrinking Labor Pool
BY RICHARD R. BECKER

As a national leader in new job creation, Las Vegas is facing the realities of the shrinking labor pool. Progressive companies are offering new Generation X workers nontraditional perks. Flexible schedules, casual dress codes, loose arrival times, and independence are among the benefits Generation X workers not only receive, but expect to receive from employers.

Some resorts offer salaries high enough to distract college graduates from pursuing professional careers; a person with a teaching degree can be found working a hotel check-in desk with a better salary than most starting teachers. Businesses that must require front-line personnel to follow company procedure to the letter are forced to turn to retired seniors. Generation Xers simply do not have patience for companies that require them to follow rigid guidelines without explanation.

As a business owner, I've adapted my management style so I can retain young, qualified professionals. I now explain "why" after every instruction. I continually give positive reinforcement and listen respectfully—even when I know the view is incorrect. If I don't, they walk, and I'm left without a replacement.

None of this surprises me. Better assignments, better pay, flexibility, and opportunities to excel—all are reasons I started my own firm five years ago. I'm not surprised because I am also part of the Generation X labor pool.

Richard Becker, 28, is the owner of Copywrite, Ink, which provides writing and consulting to ad agencies and publications. He is also a staff writer for *What's On in Las Vegas* magazine. Since 1991, hundreds of Mr. Becker's articles have appeared in local and international publications.

3 Important Questions for Managers to Ponder

1. Do I expect more than 20 hours of work for 20 hours of pay?

2. Do I have expectations of my employees that I haven't talked to them about?

3. Do I "bite the bullet" and fire an employee when his or her actions warrant it—even when I'm short on staff?

Food for Thought:

1. Many managers say they "paid their dues" when they were in their twenties by working 30 hours for 20 hours of pay. If you're expecting your employees to follow suit, you will be disappointed. Today's workers tell us they don't work for free. They *are* willing to work 20 hours for 20 hours of pay. They think it's unfair to expect more.

2. If you're assuming your employees think just like you and know your expectations—even though you've not discussed them—you are likely to have problems. Talk about your expectations.

3. One of the worst things you can do to injure employee morale is ignoring recurring behavior problems.

HOW MUCH WILL I GET PAID?

*C*harlie Fuller is the owner of a successful fast food restaurant in suburban Kansas City. About five years ago, Charlie took a buy-out option from the corporation where he had worked for more than two decades. With that money, he fulfilled a lifelong dream—owning his own business. He bought a franchise in a well-known fast food company. He is doing very well; he has had five or six $200,000 months. Although the corporation doesn't dictate his hours anymore, he's put in *lots* of them to build his business. Charlie manages the day-to-day operations of the store personally.

Charlie, in his mid-forties, is a good guy. As a matter of fact, Charlie is the kind of guy who always thought if he ever had employees reporting to him, they would be lucky—because he *is* such a good guy, and because he knows what it's like *not* to be treated well by a manager.

Not long ago, after noticing that parking was hard to come by in the quickly growing commercial area where he's located, Charlie invested in a new employee parking lot. For a few weeks, customers and staff alike put up with construction noise and dust. One afternoon after the project was finally complete, Charlie was standing out looking over the new lot, feeling particularly proud of what he'd done. As he stood there, Talmadge, one of his employees, a young man in his early twenties, rode up on his bike.

"Ya know, Boss," he said, "what we really needed here was a bike rack. Most of us ride our bikes to work."

Charlie was crushed. It seemed all he ever heard from his largely twentysomething team was cynicism. "Whatever I do, it's never enough," he grumbled to himself. Then he started thinking about his management philosophy: that the front-line worker is the true key to success . . . that involved employees are better employees . . . that ideas from the front line deserve respect.

So he responded, "You may have a good idea there. I'll tell you what, why don't you check into bike racks. Find out the best kind, do some comparison shopping, get some figures on installation, bring me back the information, and I'll consider it."

"How much will I get paid?" Talmadge asked.

For Charlie, whose frustration had been growing for the last couple of years, this was the last straw. It seemed to him that his employees were clueless about what it means to have a job and keep it . . . that they weren't willing to "go the extra mile" . . . that they were quick to jump ship when other opportunities arose . . . that they held no loyalty—let alone respect—for him, the business owner.

Shaking his head, Charlie walked wearily to his office and picked up the phone with the direct line to corporate headquarters. "You gotta help me!" he pleaded, at his wit's end. "These kids are driving me nuts. I don't understand them, and I sure as hell don't know how to get them to do a good job for me. It's like herding cats."

This story is typical of dozens I've heard from managers supervising Generation X employees—and it points to the differing work ethics of two generations.

If you reacted as I did when I first heard this minidrama, you were astounded that Talmadge would ask to be paid to look into bike racks. When I was in my twenties, I would have been thrilled to be asked to do some extra work. I desperately wanted to prove myself to my manager. I would have done virtually anything to show I had leadership ability.

But that was then. This is now.

Here's the bottom line, one you may find disturbing: Talmadge was right.

Charlie Fuller holds a different work ethic than most of his employees. He is a member of the Baby Boom generation, those born between 1946 and 1964. Charlie grew up with the message, "Ask not what your country can do for you. Ask what you can do for your country." He is part of a generation that has made a habit of giving 55 hours of work for 40 hours of pay.

If Charlie expects his twentysomething employees to hold the same work ethic, he'll be disappointed every time. This is a fast food place. Talmadge works about as hard as a human being can work for a dollar. He doesn't work for free. Researching bike racks is no real privilege.

If he's like many others in his generation—43% hold minimum-wage jobs—he struggles every week to make ends meet. He has a right to be paid for extra work and extra hours. Impressing the boss doesn't interest him. And this job isn't *the* most important thing in life. His family, his friends, and the things he does for fun are more important.

This episode is about different work ethics held by people from different generations. To begin to understand what went on here, we must delve into generational personalities.

From an Xpert

It's About Survival

BY JENNET AND EMILY HUNT

Talmadge was right! While Charlie chases his entrepreneurial dream with financial help from his former employer, Talmadge, a twentysomething employee, works fast food for minimum wage! When Charlie was in his twenties, he was securely employed and under someone's wing, while fast food jobs were reserved for Mustang-dreaming high school kids. Today, our generation is filled with young people who are prevented from fulfilling their potential. MBAs are working entry-level management jobs, college graduates are secretaries, and high school graduates are being forced to take what's left: minimum-wage jobs. With headlines of downsizing in the daily papers, our generation is inundated with the reality that companies no longer invest in their employees. While employers expect hard work and dedication, we fear a passionate investment in our jobs, because employers seldom make the long-term investment in us. We're not lazy and we're not stupid; we're just mistrustful. We invest in ourselves, not our jobs, because we're the only ones who will provide any security.

It's ironic to be criticized as a generation of cynics who aren't "willing to go the extra mile," "who have no loyalty, let alone respect," and "who are quick to jump ship when other opportunities arise." The culture we grew up in fostered and nurtured this very attitude.

As children of divorce, we came home alone every day. We learned at a very young age how to take care of ourselves—to perform the job adults used to do. As a generation, it was no longer just our parents and immediate community that raised us, it was anything and anyone who passed into our home via radio, newspapers, magazines, television, and, of course, cable TV. We both remember vividly watching a television special when we were in grade school. "The Day After" was about nuclear war. It made an indelible impression on our young minds.

We both watched our single mom juggle the overwhelming task of raising two young daughters—while working a full-time day job and a part-time night job, on an income that left us barely above poverty level. We watched and listened to news about the world we would inherit, a world with a depleted ozone layer, overcrowding, starvation, soaring divorce rates, AIDS, gangs, crime, date rape, waste, and the burden of financially supporting the largest generation to date, the Baby Boomers, without much hope that Social Security would be around for us when we reached retirement age. Thus, we learned early in life that we were inheriting a heavy burden. We consequently adapted in order to survive and meet the demands of our rapidly changing society. To do anything less would have been against our sense of survival.

Jennet and Emily Hunt are sisters. Jennet, 26, is a full-time master's degree student who aspires to teach high school English—for now. Emily, 22, is a graduate student studying geology.

Twentysomething Employees

Turn-Offs

- Pretentiousness

- Hype

- High-stress work situations

- Poor-quality products

- Ugly uniforms

- Incentive programs that are "here today/gone tomorrow"

Turn-Ons

- Job sharing, job swapping, cross-training

- A cafeteria-style benefits package

- Full status for part-time employees

- Spending time with the manager

- The potential for internal promotion

- Flexible scheduling that accommodates personal needs

- Regular staff meetings

- Feeling like they're making a difference

- A productive work atmosphere

CHAPTER FIVE

WHAT MAKES CHARLIE TICK?

Formative years: healthy economy, powerful kids, excellent schools, heroes, optimism

On the job: involvement, empowerment, participation

Today: midlife issues

*C*harlie, at 46, is typical of a whole generation of managers. By my estimates, more than 60% of all front-line managers are in their thirties and forties. Of mid- and upper-level managers, more than 75% seem to be members of the Baby Boom.

Dozens of conversations with managers in a variety of industries over the past five years have led me to believe that many misunderstandings between managers and their front-line employees are actually caused by generational differences. Since the majority of front-line workers, particularly in the service industries, are members of Generation X, and since the majority of their managers are members of the Baby Boom, I believe it makes sense to develop a richer understanding of those two generational personalities.

This section will give you a more complete picture of the Baby Boom cohort—what their formative years were like, how they changed their organizations, where they are today.

Baby Boomers grew up in the fifties and sixties. The men had
come home from World War II ready to build a new world.
The economy was the healthiest in centuries. The middle class
swelled with high employment and rising wages. In 1955, the
average American income was nearly three times what it had
been in 1940. Half of the veterans of World War II attended
college on the GI bill. The federal government subsidized home
mortgages. By the end of the decade, nine of ten homes had
television sets.

The largest generation of all time, the Baby Boom has been
compared to a pig in a python. The American culture, the python,
swallowed this huge cohort, and as it attempted to digest it, the
snake was stretched to the max at each phase. In the late 1940s,
hospitals added new wings so that expectant mothers could give
birth to the 76 million new little Boomers. In the early fifties,
suburbs rose up and were quickly filled with ranch-style homes
to house growing new families. Grade schools, junior highs, and
high schools were constructed to educate the Boom children.
Madison Avenue quickly identified this powerful generation as a
target market and pitched products—from cornflakes to Kool-
Aid—to them. 75% of all families fit the Leave-It-to-Beaver
profile, with a working dad, stay-at-home mom, and 1.5 children.

The generation was powerful from the beginning, its members
becoming trendsetters for the rest of the society. Historically, fads
start with young adults and then work their way up and down.
In the fifties, *kids* started the fads—ducktails, hula hoops, poodle
skirts, and pop beads.

Children were in the spotlight; many would say indulged. Before
World War II, prevailing wisdom about child-rearing urged a
disciplined approach. Popular behaviorist John B. Watson
advised parents not to "hug and kiss children or let them sit on
your lap." Six-month-olds were strapped to their potty seats
because the schedule said it was time for potty-training. Then

along came Dr. Benjamin Spock with a revolutionary new approach that reshaped America's concept of child care. He told parents that love and cuddling was not only acceptable—but actually contributed to the healthy development of the child.

Boomers attended schools in a system that today's educators say had hit its peak. Classes were taught by the best and brightest women—who had few other career options. In school, kids were taught to be good members of a team; on their report cards, they were graded, right alongside of their grades for math and English, for "works with others" and "shares materials with classmates."

It was a time of great expectations. Roger Bannister broke the four-minute mile. There were heroes—John Wayne, Grace Kelly, presidents, senators, athletes, and Boy Scout leaders—to look up to and emulate. People were fascinated by the western frontier. On TV, they watched Roy Rogers, Daniel Boone, Hopalong Cassidy, Gene Autrey, Dale Evans, and Davy Crockett. Sputnik sparked a fascination with space, "to boldly go where no one had gone before."

This all began to unravel in the sixties with JFK's assassination, the Cold War's escalation, and the start of the Vietnam War. But even campus protests and the civil rights movement were based on the belief that this generation could truly make a difference.

There was so much hope for the young that *Time* magazine actually gave its Man of the Year Award in 1967 to the Baby Boom Generation. It said this was the generation that would clean up our cities and find a cure for cancer and the common cold. Never before in history had youth been so idealized as they were at this time.

Even for the poor and the disenfranchised, the message was hope. The plot line promised, "A better life is right around the corner."

"Wait a minute," you may be saying, "I'm a member of this generation, but that's not the way I grew up." Yes. Clearly this is an idealized version of the Baby Boom's formative years. But this is the data that was input. This was the picture that was forming—of the way life was or, at least, the way life *should be.* It is what shaped the Boom generation's personality, and it had a tremendous impact on every member.

HOW THE BOOMERS CHANGED THE WORKPLACE

In the seventies, Baby Boomers became the majority cohort in most companies. With an economic power that surpasses the gross national product of most countries, they were used to having things their way and they became a demanding workforce—one that expected far more from an employer than had previous generations.

When Boomers first arrived on the job, most companies still operated according to a manufacturing model. Management systems tended to range from paternalism to autocracy. Management was considered the brain; the labor force, the brawn. But the Boomers wanted to work in a different kind of place. They wanted to be involved in decisions, to influence the direction their organizations would take, to have a voice.

The Boomers were generally willing to pay their dues for a few years, studying the politics of groups and learning how to get into positions where they could make a difference. By the early eighties, they were well entrenched, and they began to have a profound effect on what was happening. They were the primary force behind a new way of doing business that includes such practices as participative management, flattened pyramids, employee involvement, quality circles, team-building, and empowerment.

Today, most members of the Baby Boom are moving into their golden era, stepping into the positions and earnings they've worked so hard for all these years. Many have just purchased—or are about to purchase—that luxury item they've always wanted: the boat, vacation home, or recreation vehicle.

But life isn't rosy for all Baby Boomers. Many are facing—up close and personal—the results of re-engineering and down-sizing. They're looking for new jobs—or struggling to establish themselves as independent consultants. They worry they won't be able to make the payment on the home they financed shortly before they were "dejobbed."

All are facing significant midlife issues. How will I handle my aging parent? When will this very active parenting role I've played for so long with my own Generation X kids come to an end? Or, for those with small children at home, how will I balance child-rearing with growing my career—while maintaining my sanity?

Many are asking themselves if this might not be the right time to slow down and work a bit less, find more time for gardening, reading, and fitness—in short, a life outside of work. As they move into their early fifties, the generation that redefined "hard work" may find itself rethinking its priorities.

The Boomers Took the Big Payoff
BY ANDREW MILLER

Growing up in the seventies and eighties, we watched the rich and powerful on *Dynasty* and *Dallas*. When we turned 16, many of us had our own cars. We drove to school, football games, and parties. Many of us went straight from high school to college, expecting the big payoff and the luxuries TV had promised us. When we graduated from college, we either expected to go into graduate school or to get the job and the payoff.

But it didn't happen the way we expected. The college degree didn't mean the same thing it once did. We weren't automatically given the decent jobs we expected, nor could we necessarily go into the field we had studied for. The Baby Boomers were entrenched, and they held onto their jobs. Few places were opening for newcomers. If we found a job, advancement was limited. As we watched companies downsize and move toward using temporary or part-time employment, we had to wonder, *what about us*? Weren't we told if we went to school and worked hard, we'd get good jobs? But it didn't happen that way—and we have to wonder if we will ever have the same things our parents do.

Andrew Miller is a 29-year-old English instructor at Northern Kentucky University.

"I'm an idealist. I believe whole-heartedly in these things; I believe you can—in a society where people get divorced every five minutes—stay married for 50 years. It's been done. It's beautiful."

—Actor Johnny Depp

8 Harsh Economic Facts of Life for Twentysomethings

1. Poverty among twentysomethings has increased by 50% since the mid-1970s.

2. In the 1950s, young homeowners could make the monthly mortgage payment by using 14% of their income. Today it takes 40%.

3. Americans work an average of one month per year more than they did 20 years ago, yet real wages have steadily declined since 1973.

4. Today, folks older than 60 will get back about $200 for every $100 they put into Social Security. Twentysomethings will lose more than $100 for every $450 they contribute.

5. Home ownership may be unrealistic for many members of Generation X. The median price of a home (adjusted for inflation) has increased 78% in the last 30 years.

6. In the 1960s, one of ten college graduates took jobs that didn't require their degrees. Over the next 15 years, one in three graduates will have to settle for jobs that don't match their credentials.

7. Today a 30-year-old man can expect to earn 25% less than his dad did at the same age. By contrast, his father earned more than Grandpa did at 30.

8. Fortune 500 companies are laying off workers at an unprecedented pace. The trend is expected to worsen in the next century.

CHAPTER SIX

HOW DOES TALMADGE SEE THE WORLD?

A generation with its own unique personality

Formative years: rocky economy, the Me Decade, outdated schools, latchkey children, scandalous TV, fallen heroes, broken homes, lowered expectations

*L*et's revisit that episode in the parking lot from Chapter Four. Talmadge, the twentysomething employee, outspoken about bike racks and wages, represents a whole generation of front-line employees. By my estimates, at least 80% of all frontline workers—at least in the service industries—are in their teens and twenties, members of Generation X.

On the job: self-reliance, skepticism, financial savvy, balance, commitment reluctance, blurred life-stage boundaries, nonauthority, technology, diversity

Today: struggling to get a foothold in the adult world

If you're managing employees in their teens and twenties, it's important to realize they are members of a generation with its own unique personality. This is not "just a phase they will grow out of."

The view we hold of the world—the way it is and the way it should be—is formed, for the most part, during our first 10 to 15 years of life. This worldview is shaped by what is around us in those formative years: our family and friends, the schools we attend, the place we grow up, what's going on in the media, world events, the economy.

Its place in history—along with all the events that are part of that time—shape each generation's unique personality. Individual members of a generation are greatly influenced by the generation they are a part of. Some identify completely with their cohort's personality, exhibiting all the characteristics typical of their group; others spend a lifetime trying to live down the reputation their generation has established.

Some managers, frustrated by their twentysomething employees, tell themselves, "I was just the same when I was younger. Eventually they'll wake up and smell the coffee." If we brush off our differences as "just a phase" and expect today's young employees to "grow out of it," we'll be sorely disappointed. The workers in this new generation were raised in a very different world than the generations ahead of them. They see the world differently—especially the world of work.

As people grow older, they adjust their behaviors. They build their skills. They expand their knowledge. But they generally do not radically change the way they view the world. Most of the characteristics of the Generation X personality will remain with its members throughout their lives.

Identifying and understanding generational personalities can be tremendously valuable, especially to managers. This knowledge can help us to empathize, communicate, and motivate—in short, to be better managers.

To understand Talmadge, or any of the other 40 million employees in his age group, a good place to begin is to sharpen our picture of their formative years and to get a read on what this generation faces today—on the job market and in their personal lives.

GROWING UP IN THE SEVENTIES AND EIGHTIES

Generation X grew up in the seventies and eighties—with Watergate, Jonestown, John Travolta, and pet rocks. The war in Vietnam was grinding down to its painful conclusion. *Economically,* times were rough. The experts argued: Was it recession, inflation, stagflation, or depression? The stock market dropped 22%, almost double the record set in the 1920s. Interest rates climbed and unemployment increased. Cars lined up around the block to fill up with gasoline as the country faced a fuel crisis. To conserve energy, President Jimmy Carter announced he would forego lighting the national Christmas tree.

Disillusioned with the economy and politics, people focused on: themselves. It was the *Me Decade,* the Golden Age of Polyester. Whether they joined a health club, enrolled in a self-help group, or went on a macrobiotic diet, individuals sought to fulfill their personal goals. It was a particularly unpopular time to be a child. The initial members of Generation X were some of the first babies whom adults took pills to prevent. In the seventies, adults rated cars ahead of kids as necessary for the good life.

Kids went to *school* in a system that had grown outdated. Times had changed; children and their needs had changed; the world had changed; employers and their requirements had changed; technology had changed; knowledge itself had grown exponentially. Yet the schools had just barely begun to change. In a well-meaning effort to reproduce the success of the educational system of the fifties and sixties, schools steadfastly applied the same old formula. Operating on a harvesting calendar and an old manufacturing model (straight rows of orderly children), teachers grew increasingly frustrated as aptitude test scores plummeted and kids grew more and more unruly. Angry community members refused to support the schools with more tax dollars. By the late seventies, it was clear the system needed reform. What followed was a decade of experimentation, in which schools and teachers explored a plethora of new approaches.

Many kids came home from school in the afternoon and were on their own. Fifty percent were latchkey children. After school, they let themselves into homes that were silent. Not only were Mom and Dad not yet home from work, they were still deep in the workday, and it might be hours before they got home. There was often a note on the refrigerator. They popped snacks into the microwave—and then played Nintendo or Atari, learning early to be autonomous and take care of themselves.

Since their parents weren't home, the television became the foster parent. Certainly, the Boomers had grown up with TV— but a very different TV. Whereas the Boomers watched *Lassie* and *Leave It to Beaver* and *The Lone Ranger*—shows where the values were consistent with the ones teachers were trying to instill in the classroom—the Xers grew up with a very sophisticated television. The Boomers had network TV with three or four choices of programs; the Xers had cable, MTV, talk shows, and choices galore. They watched *Dynasty, The Jeffersons, Let's Make a Deal,* and *Dallas.* By the time they were 16, they had watched more than 16,000 murders on television and in the movies.

It was an era in which kids watched idols crumble. In 1973 and 1974 as children switched channels they passed regularly— month after month—the ongoing saga of Watergate. Investigative journalism and a globe-spanning media uncovered and publicized our national heroes' human foibles. Vice President Spiro Agnew resigned, pleading no contest to charges of income-tax evasion. In a *Playboy* interview, presidential candidate Jimmy Carter confessed to "adultery in my heart." The House of Representatives expelled Representative Michael Myers for his connection with the ABSCAM investigation; he was the first Representative expelled in more than 100 years. FBI agent Richard W. Miller was charged with espionage, the first agent ever to face such charges. Televangelists Jim Bakker and Jimmy Swaggart were shown to be far less than saints. Most devastating of all, Richard Nixon became the first U.S. president to resign from office. The American Hero was no more.

The family picture had completely changed. In the sixties, the Leave-It-to-Beaver style family (with a working dad, stay-at-home mom, and one or two children) was the norm; 75 of 100 families fit that profile. Today, 3 in 100 fit that picture. Virtually every member of Generation X was deeply affected by divorce. Fifty percent watched their own parents divorce; the others watched helplessly as an aunt's and uncle's relationship—or the marriage of their best friend's parents—dissolved. Most will tell you they still feel the pain today.

Perhaps the most important thing about their first 10 to 15 years was the set of expectations surrounding them. Whereas the message we gave our children in the fifties and sixties was, "You can be anything you want to be—even the president," the message of the seventies and eighties was, "Be careful out there." This is the first generation that has been told it probably will be not be able to improve on—even to replicate—their parents' lifestyle.

TWENTYSOMETHING TODAY

Today, members of the X Generation are in their teens and twenties. If you ask, they will tell you that, yes, they watched the Baby Boomers work really, really hard. They watched their parents plod through 60-hour work weeks—and struggle with difficult bosses—and bring home work on the weekends. Many will tell you they watched their mother try desperately to be Supermom, juggling career, child-rearing, homemaking, and a personal life. They'll tell you most of the people they know in their thirties and forties are workaholics, that they have defined themselves by the work they do. And they will tell you *with conviction* they want a lifestyle with more balance, that they want to work to live—not live to work.

Meanwhile, most are having a hard time just making ends meet. They have friends with college degrees working what they call "McJobs" and buddies with PhDs driving taxis. Still others haven't been able to find work at all. More than 22 million have moved back home because they can't pay the rent . . . and feed themselves . . . and make the car payment . . . on the money they're making.

THE GEN X WORK ETHIC

All of this translates into a generation of workers with a different work ethic than most managers. Here are the main components of that work ethic:

Self-Reliance

Having learned to fend for themselves as children, twentysomething workers tend to be autonomous. On the job, they sometimes think of themselves as free agents or contractors. Group-oriented Baby Boom managers find this attitude frustrating. They sometimes interpret it as disloyalty. It is true that Generation Xers don't give away their loyalty easily.

Skepticism

When they look around at the world and what they're inheriting, it can be overwhelming: pollution, crime, racial tension, AIDS. In the face of all this, twentysomethings often feel powerless. Managers label them "jaded"—and say they don't find the optimism in their younger employees they themselves felt when they were new in the workforce.

The Need for a Bridge

Financial Savvy

On their own as children, they were often given money to pay the plumber or buy a gallon of milk. Today, whether they're pinching pennies to pay the rent or buying hundred-dollar tennis shoes, twentysomethings know how far a dollar goes.

Many people have labeled them materialistic. In truth, most just want to get out of debt. They will inherit the worst public debt in U.S. history. Surveys show teens worry they won't have enough money when they grow up.

On the job, they tend to think of themselves as marketable commodities. Show them how you're helping them become more marketable, and you're more likely to get what you want in return.

Balance

When Larry Bradford and I wrote *Twentysomething* (Merrill-Alexander, 1992), virtually every young person we interviewed told us, "My parents are workaholics, and I want none of it." These people don't want to sacrifice for a job. The job is often not their number-one priority. They want time—for a life away from work.

Commitment Reluctance

For this generation, there is a reluctance to commit—both personally and professionally. The marriage age is the highest of the century: 25 for women and 27 for men. Professionally, people are waiting to make a commitment. After six years on the job, one "blue chip" employee announced on a Monday morning, "I just decided to make this a career." His manager was shocked. He had assumed all along this young man was in it for the long haul.

Blurred Life-Stage Boundaries

For most members of Generation X, it's hard to say when childhood ended . . . when adolescence was over . . . when adulthood began. Many believe Generation Xers were robbed of their childhood by the responsibilities they took on as children and by the media.

Sociologists tell us that adolescence no longer ends at age 20, that socially and developmentally, adolescence now extends into the twenties. And remember the four-year college degree? It now takes an average of five and a half years to complete. Then there's a huge wave of what are called "boomerang kids," young adults who have returned home to live with Mom and Dad.

When do Xers become adults? They're having a hard time getting a foothold there. The typical hallmarks of adulthood—marriage, the purchase of a home, a "real" job—are eluding many of them.

For managers, this is an important issue to keep in mind. Generation X feels robbed of time with their parents. Sixty-four percent say they'll spend more time with their own kids than their parents did with them. Managers inherit life issues that weren't resolved in families. The manager now becomes the parent, and this is a generation that values time.

One executive told me last summer one of his best young managers was leaving the company. "Why?" he asked the young man. The response: "You never have any time for me."

Nonauthority

In the sixties, there was a lot of talk about being antiauthority. In contrast, members of Generation X are not particularly interested in authority. They're unimpressed by titles. They watched heroes deposed and learned early on that their parents had flaws—some of them pretty serious.

A franchise owner told me the founder of the company recently visited her shop. He asked one of her young employees how she was doing and the woman responded, "Well, a little hungover this morning, but okay." His title meant nothing to her.

Many twentysomething employees are not motivated by promotion into management; they're not certain it's something they would want to do. And they definitely won't show respect to someone just because their title is "director," "foreman," or "vice president."

Technology

Whereas the Boomers were the first to grow up with television, the Xers were the first computer generation. My favorite cartoon is from the book *13th Gen* by Neil Howe and Bill Strauss (Vintage Books, 1993). It shows two young men in a tank in the Persian Gulf War. One is reassuring the other, "No sweat. I used to play this at Chuck E. Cheese." And he's right! With complete comfort, he would probably experiment with the computer until he figured out just what to do.

On the job, twentysomething personnel are baffled or irritated by those who aren't technically literate and by businesses with systems and equipment that aren't up-to-date.

Diversity

This is the most diverse generation the United States has produced. One in three belongs to an ethnic minority, compared to one in four in the total population.

Within the generation, there are all sorts of sets and subsets. Some call themselves "slackers"—twentysomethings to whom work is a four-letter word. Some call themselves Generation E for "Entrepreneur"—people who became millionaires by age 25. There are differences between those who grew up in the Midwest and those who grew up in the East—between those from the suburbs and those from the inner city.

What's important to keep in mind is that each member of the generation is an individual, unique and different—and that the generalizations we make can only be used to *initiate* a better understanding of one another.

Although the nine traits listed so far can be seen as both positive and negative, there are some contributions Generation X brings to the workforce that are distinctive—traits they have that definitely must be listed on the assets side of the ledger.

We've already talked about their *autonomy* and their *techno-ease.* We can add *flexibility* to the list. Many packed up and moved to Dad's (or Mom's) for weekends and holidays—a different house and bedroom, a whole new neighborhood—and they learned to accept and adapt to change. Their *comfort with authority* allows them to speak up with fresh ideas since they're not seeking approval from those in charge. This *outspokenness* is important to companies striving to stay on the cutting edge.

If you review the latest business books addressing the kind of employee needed in the new economy, you will find many of these same characteristics: independent people who don't accept the status quo, who are adaptable, who embrace change, who don't expect their companies to take care of them. Members of Generation X may be the ones who are best-equipped to lead us into the twenty-first century.

From an Xpert

It's Really Quite Simple

BY TY HUTCHINSON

As I read your definition of what twentysomethings are, I again realize that no matter how much research you do on us or the thousands of questions you ask, you'll never understand. All you're doing is simply reporting what you hear and see. It's the same load of crap every other Boomer trying to capture the definition of twentysomething writes. I laugh in your face. You are so clueless. What you're writing is somewhat true, but seriously distorted. Almost so a Boomer can make sense of it.

I was a latchkey kid who came home to a silent home and fixed my own snacks. I watched my parents divorce, although I didn't quite understand. I did know that Dad no longer lived with us, and we were now poor, but Mom did her best. What did I learn from this? Duh . . . Not to divorce. I intend to have a normal Brady Bunch family, and I will take the time to plan seriously so it does happen. And it will.

Planning. That's really what I've learned. Taking the time to think things out. Maybe we're not putting off commitments, but simply devising a strategy. God forbid we repeat the stupid things our parents did. When I was growing up, I learned what *not* to do.

Some of us are screwed up, I admit that, but don't classify our entire generation as a bunch of misfits. Most people my age are very committed to work—maybe not to a company, but definitely to the work. We have to be, if we want the good life.

So stop putting all these lame statistics gathered by a bunch of so-called authorities in books. They mean nothing to us and everything to you. Stop analyzing and trying to find an answer. The world has changed; therefore, people are going to change. It's really quite simple.

Ty Hutchinson is a 28-year-old copywriter. He lives in Los Angeles, where he has worked in advertising for five years.

3 Generations

	Traditionalist born before 1946	*Baby Boomer* born 1946–1960	*Twentysomething* born 1960–1980
Outlook:	practical	optimistic	skeptical
Work Ethic:	dedicated	driven	balanced
View of Authority:	respectful	love/hate	unimpressed
Leadership by:	hierarchy	consensus	competence
Relationships:	self-sacrifice	personal gratification	reluctance to commit
Perspective:	civic-minded	team-oriented	self-reliant

CHAPTER SEVEN

WHAT HAPPENED TO THE WORK ETHIC?

Fifty years of increasing work hours

Driven Baby Boomers

Generation X: witnessing heavy costs, waiting for "the good job," questioning the wisdom of loyalty

Something interesting happened in the postwar years. We began to work harder. For the previous 100 years, work hours decreased steadily. Then in 1948, they began to increase. And they've increased steadily. In a well-documented book (*The Overworked American: The Unexpected Decline of Leisure,* BasicBooks, 1991), Harvard economist Juliet Schor reports that time spent on the job in a given year has increased by 163 hours in the last 20 years. That's an extra month per year! She tells us working mothers average more than 80 hours of work a week between their jobs, housework, and childcare. Leisure time has decreased by one-third. One overzealous CEO requires anyone who works for him to have a phone in the bathroom. Meanwhile, productivity has increased steadily. Today it takes us half the time to produce what was produced in the average work week 50 years ago.

Working until midnight . . . going for months without a day off . . . taking work home . . . moonlighting . . . going into the office on Saturdays and Sundays . . . cutting down on sleep . . . juggling work and family . . . rushing . . . hurrying . . . feeling pulled in all directions—these are the behaviors many companies reward. And these are the hallmarks of the Baby Boom lifestyle. Perhaps it made sense for Boomers, who have always sought desperately for approval, to sacrifice for a job. Mostly, their sacrifices paid off.

When it comes to Generation X, it's a different story. They have witnessed their parents' heart attacks, high blood pressure, depression, and divorce. They have watched the downsizing, delayering, and layoffs. They believe their parents are literally working themselves to death—and they're quite sure it simply isn't worth it. Patently pragmatic, twentysomethings recognize that there's no longer any such thing as job security. The new economy and the huge size of the Baby Boom generation have translated into much longer transitions into a "good job." Members of the X Generation want jobs that pay well, are not terribly stressful, and end when the workday is over. They believe that work should not be more important than their friends, families, and hobbies. One friend recently told me, "If you want loyalty, get a dog."

It's not that Generation X lacks a work ethic. It's just that they've witnessed firsthand a work ethic that eats people up and spits them out—and they want something different.

In many other countries (Australia and the United Kingdom, for example), most entry-level workers *begin* with four to six weeks of vacation per year. Visitors from these countries are often astounded at the miserly vacation leave typical of most American companies.

Interestingly enough, as the front edge of the Baby Boom begins to turn 50, we're beginning to hear some of the same themes from them. Many are recognizing that they've given their lives to their work while neglecting to build significant relationships with their families. They worry that when it comes time to retire, they may find themselves without anything meaningful to do—or anyone meaningful to do it with.

Perhaps, between the pressure exerted by twentysomething workers and the quest for a more balanced lifestyle by aging Boomers, companies may redefine "work ethic" and change their expectations of employees. The Eddie Bauer company in Chapel Hill, North Carolina, has done just that. It wants its people to lead balanced lives. "We don't want them to mistake having a career with having a life," says one executive. In addition to three days of personal leave per year, all employees are now eligible for one "Balance Day" per month. Company leaders believe they'll be paid back in increased loyalty. Turnover has already decreased.

Examples such as this are a hopeful sign that we may soon quit "working people to death." Yet, as businesses grow leaner, placing heavier work loads on fewer people with fewer resources—and the marketplace grows more and more competitive—it is hard to give a hopeful prognosis for the work ethic.

Generation X is not alone in calling for more balance. As the Boomers enter their fifties and people of all ages grow more aware of overwork issues, the generations may find they have moved toward a shared perspective on work and leisure.

Balancing Career and Family
BY JENNY ARNSPARGER

When I was growing up, my parents juggled my brother and me around. They were always shifting their schedules to make sure we were taken care of. I remember daycare places and babysitters. One parent would stay with my brother and me while the other traveled. My mom was always hopping from one plane to another, and many nights my dad worked until nine.

I always thought, "I'm going to balance career and family." I want to be there for my kids, not only for their most important moments, but for everyday experiences. I want to travel *with* my family. I don't want to give up hobbies and other things I enjoy.

The place I work sells fun and recreation. Because of that, people are a lot more relaxed about spending time with family, exercising, and doing things outdoors. During the busy season, hours are long, and the work load is extremely heavy. However, because of rewards such as occasional parties, good deals on recreational activities, and pats on the back, we are more than happy to put in a little extra effort. Although there are a couple of people who are always there bright and early and don't leave until everyone else is gone, for the most part, the attitude is "work hard and play hard."

Jenny Arnsparger, a 23-year-old speech communications graduate, works as a receptionist for Volant, Inc., manufacturers of skis and snowboards.

"I find it interesting that a family-focused business scoffs when you want to take a day off to spend time with your family."

—Jennet Hunt, Graduate Student, Age 26

Generation X:
Truth and Fiction

STEREOTYPE:	*REALITY:*
• Slacker	• Some slackers, lots of hard workers, some superachievers
• Doesn't have to work	• 43% earning minimum wage; many struggling to survive
• Has lived on "Easy Street"; "handed everything on a silver platter"	• Many took on adult responsibilities as children; many grew up in single-parent families

CHAPTER EIGHT

ARE YOU THE PARENT?

irst—and most important—it's not your fault.

Feelings of guilt

If you blame yourself for not spending enough time with your kids when they were growing up, if you feel guilty for working too many hours away from home, if you feel bad about not holding the marriage together for the kids' sake, give it up. You did the best you could under the circumstances.

Parents with good intentions

There were so many of us competing for the good jobs that it made sense to work as hard as we could. The economy had changed; you probably couldn't have managed on just one salary. Everybody was divorcing, and they seemed better for having made the change. It was the 1970s—"gotta be free; gotta be me." Folks were into EST, codependency groups, and the New Age.

It's not too late

We certainly had good intentions. Our generation was certain we were going to be the best parents ever. None of those sugary, nutritionless cereals in our homes. No guns in the toy box. We would respect our children's individuality and humanity in wonderful new ways. We would establish open communication so our kids would feel safe talking to us about anything.

Now we see we weren't the perfect parents—that, as a matter of fact, many of our choices caused pain for our children.

If you are a parent of someone in his or her teens or twenties, here are some of the issues you face today:

✗ We have a very different relationship with our kids than our parents had with us. Most Baby Boomers saw their parents as authority figures. They may not have been afraid of them exactly, but there was a distance there, a certain respect. Members of Generation X learned early on that Mom and Dad were human and fallible. The parent-child relationship has tended to be much more egalitarian, with kids treating their parents like friends who happen to be a bit older.

✗ Kids in their twenties are returning home in droves to live with their parents. Called "boomerang kids," they're finding they can't make ends meet on their meager salaries, and they're moving back in. Besides, they never got enough time with their parents when they were younger. Why not now?

✗ Many parents with children in their twenties are asking themselves, "When is this active parenting role I've played for so long going to end?" With the Baby Boomers' parents, the parental role shifted when they were in their twenties; parents gradually became less actively involved in their offspring's lives.

✗ The role the Baby Boom parent has played probably will *not* change. Since you've treated each other like equals for so long, your kids probably see no need to change the relationship. They are likely to continue to come to you for advice, support, friendship, mentoring, time—yes, even money—as long as you're available.

✗ The American Dream doesn't sparkle anymore. The experts tell us Generation X will not be able to replicate our lifestyle. As mentors of today's twentysomethings, parents are hard-pressed to know how to advise their young offspring who are trying so hard to get a foothold in the adult world.

It's a tough time to be a parent. Yet you're as important as ever. You're needed desperately—as a guide, supporter, friend, and cheerleader.

What can you do?

1. Accept that it's different today. Don't impose your view of the world. Bite your tongue when you start to say, "When *I* was in *my* twenties. . . ."

2. Be cautiously optimistic. Parents who cling to an outdated picture of the American Dream and sell it to their young adult offspring will only create heartbreak. Educate yourself about the realities young people face today—particularly in finding satisfying work. (I recommend reading *Late Bloomers: Coming of Age in Today's America: The Right Place at the Wrong Time,* by David Lipsky and Alexander Abrams, Times Books, 1994.) But pessimism won't help either. Assist your twentysomethings in shaping realistic goals and encourage them along the way as they achieve them.

3. If you haven't had a good relationship, it's not too late to start. They need you now. Jump in and give it a try.

4. Come clean. If you didn't do a good job as a parent, talk to your offspring about your failings.

5. Spend time together—doing almost anything. Remember this is a generation that feels they were robbed of time with their parents. Your time is a valuable gift.

6. Be a great listener.

7. Help your son or daughter to explore options. Be creative. This generation will be called upon to find new alternatives to living economically, to finding job satisfaction.

8. Don't get caught in the trap of thinking, "If we could just go back to the good old days, things would be fine." We can't go back. The world has changed. We are in a transitional time and it is often chaotic, frequently confusing. It's hard to know exactly what's ahead, but a new future awaits us. There will be new models for working and for parenting, and it is our twentysomething kids who will help create them.

From an pert

There's Simply Not a Flight That Goes There Anymore
BY JIM HUNT

I am the 53-year-old father of two twentysomething women. From my current perspective, I would challenge and change, if I could, dozens of choices I made as a parent. I would not, however, trade—for anything in the world, the chance to have experienced fatherhood. My lovely, liberal, brilliant, outspoken daughters are the pride and honor of my life.

For years I've had a theory that no matter what we do as parents, we screw up our kids. I also believe that, although our kids may not listen to what we *say,* they do monitor and respond to what they see us *do.* Frequently, they make our patterns—both constructive and destructive—their own. At other times our patterns serve as countermodels, and our kids resort to extreme measures and escape to places where we could not possibly follow. I have no trouble understanding tattoos and piercings and membership in cults. "They can't follow me here," some of them must declare with relief.

Although my daughters have no unusual tattoos or piercings, I recently asked a twentysomething co-actor in a play to help me understand her body markings in terms of her future. Melanie's response still haunts me: "First of all," she said, "I like them. And if I change my mind later, I can always have the tattoos removed and let the piercings close up. Truth is, though, I really don't expect to live all that long."

My guess is that very few Xers (unless they have parents with lots of money or trust funds that allow them to live as if the world hadn't changed) have a particularly compelling picture of even the path they want to be on, let alone the goal at the end of it. I see today's young people struggling to find ways to feel even slightly secure, to find ways to even want to continue the journey, when many of the destinations they grew up thinking they might travel to have been deleted from the screen.

My daughters earned their undergraduate degrees either on or ahead of schedule. Both are now in graduate school, without help from their mother or me, because they found out almost immediately that the fields they had studied (English and Geology) offered them no career opportunities. They're not hiding out in graduate school; on the contrary, they're using their creativity and hard-learned flexibility to try to construct something that will allow them more choices in a world where they absolutely have to invest in and take care of themselves.

In my mind, hope lies in the possibility that today's twentysomethings will be the ones who—like the phoenix rising from the ashes—get to design a 21st century that embraces chaos and change, and that creates fresh new infrastructures, that shapes new systems, that brings the world together.

In the meantime, I am thrilled to still be a valued part of their process. Nothing pleases me more than a phone call from one or both of my grown women kids: "Hi, Dad. You got time for a cup of coffee?" Today, of course, this means a tall, skinny, hazelnut latté with extra foam.

Jim Hunt is the founder and owner of The Write Idea, an internationally recognized communication consortium that specializes in business writing and presentation skills.

HOW TO BUILD THE BRIDGE

188 Tips, Tools, and Tactics

The Best Boss

". . . gets to know me personally."

". . . is sincere."

". . . shows appreciation."

". . . is fun."

". . . is usually relaxed."

". . . is people-oriented."

". . . gives me regular feedback on my performance."

HOW TO BUILD THE BRIDGE

188 Tips, Tools, and Tactics

WHAT GENERATION X WORKERS WANT FROM THEIR MANAGERS

So how can you translate what you've read so far into your day-to-day life on the job? What do these young employees want? If we're designing management systems based on their values and needs, how do we proceed? What kind of work environments attract, retain, and motivate Generation X?

I recently facilitated focus groups of twentysomething workers in five cities across the United States. We had diverse groups: urban and rural, inner-city and suburban, multiethnic. I was amazed at how consistently they answered when asked what they want from their managers.

Here are their seven most frequent requests:

✗ Appreciate us.

✗ Be flexible.

✗ Create a team.

✗ Develop us.

✗ Involve us.

✗ Lighten up.

✗ Walk your talk.

I call these the X Requisites for managers.

Now, you may be asking yourself, "Does she think this stuff is rocket science?" Obviously not. But these are the issues that are important to this group of workers; this is what they want—and they will tell you *with feeling* that these principles are not practiced in most places they've worked.

A note about the importance of these practices: 10 years ago, had we discussed managing young workers, we might have agreed that doing these things would be nice—perhaps even the right thing to do. Here is today's reality: if you are managing a business or a team where the majority of your front-line workers are members of the X Generation, your business *will not survive* unless you manage them well. It's that simple. Poorly treated employees perform poorly. Well-treated employees perform well. Managing with excellence is *mandatory* in today's highly competitive business environment.

The remainder of this book delves into the seven X Requisites. Each is explained fully: what it means, why it's important to Generation X. Then you will find at least a dozen case studies, proven strategies, and low-cost ideas for implementing each practice.

Don't let these suggestions overwhelm you. If you did all of these things, it would be too much. I hope you will come back to this section again and again to find innovative ideas that will help you become a more successful manager.

"People my age are working four different jobs. They're playing them off against each other and bucking the system."

—Emily Hunt, Graduate Student, Age 22

The 7 X Requisites

The Most Frequent Requests
Generation Xers Make of Their Managers

1. *Appreciate us.* Show you care.

2. *Be flexible.* Let us have a life beyond work.

3. *Create a team.* Give us the family we never had.

4. *Develop us.* Help us to increase our skills.

5. *Involve us.* Ask our opinions.

6. *Lighten up.* Remember, it's not brain surgery.

7. *Walk your talk.* Practice what you preach.

CHAPTER ONE

APPRECIATE US

*A*lthough everyone appreciates recognition, young workers desperately want and need to know when they've done something well. I consistently hear from younger workers, "I really wish I knew *someone* appreciated what I do here."

Recognition is not commonplace in business today. We get too busy to acknowledge our people and we assume they know they've done a good job. Some managers ask, "Why do I have to thank them at all? Their paycheck is their reward."

A paycheck isn't enough anymore.

James Autry, author of *Love and Profit* and former Fortune 500 executive, wrote many personal notes to employees over the years. When one of his people won $5,000 in the lottery, he wrote her a note of congratulations and added, "I hope you won't take your earnings and leave us. We need you here." Years later, at his retirement, she approached him with tears in her eyes. "I'll never forget that note you wrote me," she said. Our words are powerful, and they often stay with others for a lifetime.

Appreciation is ultimately an *attitude.* It will be reflected in the way you speak to and listen to your people.

In addition, here is a batch of strategies for recognizing twenty-something employees. Of course, you will need to select the strategies that fit your work culture and your personal style. Then, even more important, you will want to choose the type of recognition that fits the individual.

✗ Go out of your way to thank someone who has done a good job. Privately? In front of others? Both!

✗ Give a half-day off for high performance. Freedom and time are important to Generation Xers.

> At the Plaza Hotel in New York City, supervisors are required to thank each member of their staff at the end of every shift for something specific the employee did that day.

> At Fazoli's Italian restaurants, the Employee of the Month is sent for a "glamour shot"—to one of those studios that give you a makeover and then take a photo in which you look fabulously glitzy. The photos are hung in the foyer. The managers report their workers love it. (You might think this award appropriate for the women only, but the Fazoli's people say the men enjoy the glamour-shot experience as much or more.)

✗ Handwrite a card. Personalize it. Be specific. Be genuine.

✗ Find out about people's personal interests (bike racing, fishing, movies, theater, music, motocross). Customize the reward to fit the receiver.

✗ Make a special point of repeating information to an employee when another manager compliments you about one of your people.

The standard preshift meeting at Marie Callender's restaurants is outlined on a form used by managers to plan the daily meetings. A routine part of the meeting is the "Great Job" section, in which the manager pinpoints the actions of a specific individual from the previous business day.

The canopy over the employee entrance at the Doubletree Hotel in St. Louis reads, "V.I.P. ENTRANCE." The sign next to the door says, "Through this door pass the most dedicated hotel employees in St. Louis. You *are* the best. Thank you for being here!"

✗ To celebrate a team success, bring in ice cream or frozen yogurt bars for everybody.

✗ Consider giving coupons for fast food to young workers trying to live on a shoestring.

✗ Have a star performer's car washed in the parking lot.

To deal with the problem of employees not showing up for work, one of the Kroger's grocery stores gives employees $100 savings bonds for showing up 30 days in a row.

✗ Give movie passes.

✗ Get to know each of your employees as an individual. What motivates one will be different from what motivates another.

✗ When someone has done a good job, ask the whole crew to give that person a standing ovation; who wouldn't love it?

A department store in Denver has a clearly marked "Employee of the Month" parking space right outside the front entry. It is visible to customers and co-workers.

✗ Give tickets to a concert or a game.

✗ Give a top performer a big button that says, "I'm a star!"

✗ Catch people in the act of doing a good job . . . and say something right then.

✗ Give an employee an actual pat on the back. It just might make someone's day.

✗ Give a coupon for a CD (I had "compact disc" in mind, but if a "certificate of deposit" is in the budget, so much the better!).

✗ Take employees out for a cup of coffee on their one-month anniversary.

✗ Send birthday cards to everyone on your staff.

✗ Unsure about how to reward your employees? Ask them. One of the worst mistakes you can make is to make decisions *for* them. In the mid-1980s, one well-known electronics company awarded its outstanding salespeople—mostly women—with a gift certificate for Sharper Image products, which in those years, were primarily for men. The women felt more disregarded than rewarded.

✗ If you institute a recognition program—Employee of the Month or a certification system—*stick with it*. Young employees claim we're not consistent and we practice a "fad of the month" management style.

Appreciation = Listening to Me
BY DAWN M. LOMBARD

I have been told I am too outspoken for a person of my age. Granted, I have less experience in the business world than my more seasoned co-workers, but if we all think alike, no one is truly thinking. In this respect, I have gone against the norm in my current company and have offered suggestions and opinions. For the most part, my input has been ignored and ridiculed.

I have now reached a point where I do not bother trying to be innovative. This is truly a shame since we twentysomethings are the people who will be running these very companies in the future. How can we perform when we are given no praise, guidance, or respect?

If my suggestions are off-base, give me the courtesy of telling me personally. Let me know why I am wrong and what a better suggestion might have been.

Some people are so set in their ways that they are not willing to do anything but what has always been done. How can companies grow and improve if their employees are stagnant?

As a Generation Xer, I simply want to be validated. This would be the greatest form of appreciation I could receive from my boss. Material items mean nothing to me; I am no longer a child. Please, respect my opinion and listen. You had faith in me the day you hired me; have faith that one of my quirky suggestions might actually make the company more successful.

Dawn M. Lombard, 24, is a product manager for an international direct mail publisher. Dawn lives in Derby, Connecticut.

Twentysomethings' Most Common Complaints About Baby Boom Managers

"They spend too much time and energy trying to figure out just what to say to whom and when, in order to get ahead."

'They are self-righteous about their generation and what it has accomplished."

"They say one thing, then do another."

"They have been harsh in their judgment of my generation."

"They're totally caught up in their Yuppie world."

CHAPTER TWO

BE FLEXIBLE

*B*eing an outstanding manager requires an appreciation for differences. Each member of the X Generation is unique—with a different background and a different way of approaching the job. Instead of passing judgment on what's right and wrong, good and bad, acceptable and unacceptable, successful managers value the unique contributions of each of their people.

Practically speaking, this valuing of differences causes the effective manager to administer policies and schedules with an eye for how they affect each individual. For example, a working mother going to night school will have different scheduling needs than a single up-and-comer hungry for hours and honors.

Young workers consistently tell me that work is important to them—but it's not their #1 priority. They have strong outside interests—school, hobbies, family, social activities. They want balance in their lives.

69

✗ Keep a bulletin board in a central location, and post photos of your staff off-the-job (with their children and friends, playing soccer, at graduation).

✗ Be as flexible with the schedule as you can. When it doesn't interfere with getting the job done, allow employees to come in an hour earlier so they can get away for the soccer game or to pick up the kids from day care. Let people swap shifts as long as it is clear to you who is working when.

✗ Use a light touch with the policy manual.

✗ If an employee doesn't fit the standards for your dress code, ask yourself if it's a safety or health risk. If not, pull together a team that includes the employee in question. Discuss your company's goals and your typical customer to see what the impact of the dress issue might be. See if the issue can be resolved in a way that makes sense to everyone, especially the employee involved.

> Microsoft encourages employees to ride their bikes to work—and, to make it practical, the company provides showers and lockers.

> At Walt Disney World, cast members get a certain number of personal days—rather than sick days—per year. That way, if they celebrate a holiday that isn't on the company calendar, they don't have to call in "sick." They just let their manager know they'll be taking a personal day.

✗ Allow discussion among your staff about controversial topics. Coach them to listen and learn from divergent perspectives.

✗ Make certain your staff's ethnic profile correlates with your customer base—and with the neighborhood where your business is located.

How To Build the Bridge

Mosby Great Performance sells a set of handsome posters for the workplace called "The Diversity Collection." Each poster includes a personal story and a striking portrait. For example, one shows a photo of a Mexican-American anthropologist. The text begins, "Growing up in East Oakland, our family life was centered around Mexican cultural traditions—language, food, religion. . . ." (For more information, call 1-800-433-3803.)

✗ Be sensitive about religious holidays. Your staff may include people with a variety of beliefs.

✗ Update your policy manual. Does it, for example, prohibit earrings for men? Unless there is a safety issue, the policy might need to be re-examined.

Since Promus Hotels never close, employees are given P.T.O.—paid time off. Instead of vacation and sick-leave days, all of it gets lumped together. Employees earn the P.T.O. and then take the time off when they want to. They are required to take *some* time off every year—at least 10 days—but the company will buy back P.T.O. if employees prefer the cash.

✗ Offer cafeteria-style benefit packages. While a great 401 (k) program may not have much appeal to some Xers, they may get excited about being able to "buy" an extra week of vacation.

✗ Learn to see issues from employees' unique perspectives.

At Bell Northern Research, the research and development arm of NORTEL, the "campus" never closes. So, if the creative juices are flowing at 2:00 A.M., employees can stick with their project. The company seeks to provide conveniences that make this lifestyle easier. Employees can leave their cleaning at the convenience store in the lobby. An automatic teller machine is available. The company hosts more than 30 recreation groups—from the amateur radio club to a parent's group.

As a result of legal problems about the dismissal of an employee who would not work on Sundays, Wal-Mart is training managers in religious harassment and civil rights—and how to accommodate employees' religious beliefs.

At the AlphaGraphics print shop in Nogales, Arizona, a young saleswoman was struggling with child visitation issues. Her former husband had custody of their four-year-old son, and she had been given visitation privileges. Not only was it difficult to schedule visits so they didn't interfere with her work requirements, but she worried she didn't have a suitable place to bring the child. Owners Gary and Aida Cooper created a play area with a VCR and videotapes in the store—and even encouraged their employee to take the child on sales calls with her.

T.G.I. Friday's has instituted a program designed to complement the lifestyle of this highly mobile generation by giving them the flexibility to visit other cities and still go to work. Company passports, which are valid for six months, give employees traveling to other cities entree into all T.G.I. Friday's restaurants. Hundreds of employees take advantage of the program each year.

Starbucks recognizes that part-time employees are critical to its success. A recent new policy states that after 90 days, employees who work at least 20 hours per week are eligible for benefits, training, and even company ownership. Company president Howard Schultz says Starbucks wants to create a "stakeholder corporation." He reports that since the policy was instituted, the attrition rate has declined dramatically.

✗ Ask your people to educate you about themselves—what it was like where they grew up, what's important in their family and culture.

✗ Make certain your staff feels that it's safe to speak up. Have an open door policy, and honor it.

✗ If you're older than 30, remember that it's a different world today from when you were in your twenties. It is no longer safe to assume that what was true for you when you were a young worker is also true for the people you manage.

✗ You're much more likely to attract and retain good twenty-something workers if you're open to scheduling options such as job sharing.

From an pert

On Navel Rings and Eggplant-Colored Hair
BY ELIZABETH CLAIRE

I want flexibility when it comes to "who I am." I am a 26-year-old staff assistant in the marketing division of a relatively conservative company. I have two tattoos and eleven piercings—ten in my ears, one in my navel. Depending on my mood, my hair ranges from an inch long to shoulder length. Since I respect the company, I maintain a relatively conservative appearance. I no longer dye my hair the color of eggplants—and I've taken to wearing only two of my earrings. My personal preference would be to wear all my earrings, my Doc Marten's, a baggy pair of jeans, and boxer shorts.

You won't be surprised to hear I'm thought of around the office as "the crazy one." I'm as close to Generation X as many of these people will ever get. So, every once in a while, some curious party will question me about "why I would do such a thing to myself." (It seems to me that tattoos, piercings, and very short hair on women are the main focus of the older generation's discontent.)

My last manager was 15 years older and respectful enough of me to have an interest in my life outside the office. He constantly questioned why I did the things I did. Yet, he did it in such a way that I knew he was genuinely confused and curious. He never made me feel out of place in our business unit, and I came to be the one with the wealth of knowledge about the world out there as it is now—instead of the world he remembered. (It is amusing when your boss needs your advice on a problem he's having with his children.)

My manager realized my lifestyle and the things I'm involved in could bring an entirely different perspective to our business efforts. He appreciated my unique knowledge instead of passing judgment on something he didn't understand. I am lucky to have

tially his curiosity about and acceptance of my lifestyle
romotion. I'll be proud to show him the new tattoo I'm
he hard work.

Elizabeth Clairey's friends call her "Brytain." She would like to be an actress, writer, and photographer. Brytain has been writing since the age of five, and her crowning glory will be when she can publish her photo-essay, "The Life and Times of a Sexuality Junkie." She says, "I keep my eyes and mind open in hopes of doing everything at least once." She lives in New Jersey.

Generation X's Preferred Work Environment

- Casual, friendly

- Neat, clean, orderly

- Technologically up-to-date

- Collegial

- A place to learn

- High level of freedom

- Functional, efficient

CHAPTER THREE

CREATE A TEAM

*M*any twentysomethings did not grow up in supportive, tight-knit families. Many yearn to find a "family" on the job—"family" in the best sense of the word: a group of individuals who support and encourage each other and who value each others' unique contributions.

> At one Wendy's store, a part-time employee brought in her prom dress to see what her manager thought of it.
>
> At an inner-city Chicago Wendy's, the manager knows all of his employees personally, including the names of all their family members. The crew considers the store a focus in their lives, and they come in for lunch and to "check in" on their days off.

✗ Show an interest in your people. Learn *about* them. If you're baffled by the fads, study them—on TV, in the movies, in magazine ads, in conversations. It will keep you young!

✗ Give your staff an opportunity to develop as a team—occasionally, without you. Step away from the job and leave them in charge. Later, debrief with everyone: How did it go? What could be done better next time?

✗ Pull a team together to explore a possible community service project.

✗ If the schedule and budget allow, pull everybody off the job to focus on teamwork for a few hours or a day. Participate in an outdoor ropes course activity. Go bowling. Paint an elderly person's home.

✗ Be careful about singling out just one or two of your outstanding employees. Make sure to let each person know you value him or her individually.

At Alfalfa's Market, an upscale natural foods grocery chain, staff members wear huge, handmade nametags with cartoons and fun letters that reflect the personality of the wearer.

✗ Sponsor a softball team. If your staff prefers hackysack, host a hackysack tournament.

✗ Use team language. Call them "the team." Let them know you'll be "coaching" them. Let them know it will take all of them to reach the "goal."

✗ Pull a team together to focus on how to make the customer feel part of the family.

✗ Hold regular staff meetings. I found them to be at the top of the list of requests to management in twentysomething focus groups. Nothing is more important to the development of the team than a forum in which people can learn about business priorities and work through problems together. Monthly is okay. Weekly is great. (If the schedule and the budget prohibit regular meetings, consider inviting everyone to come in an hour early three or four times a year, without pay, for coffee, donuts, and a business update.)

> Kinko's, "America's ubiquitous branch office," has very low turnover in its 700 stores. Nobody at Kinko's is an "employee." They're "co-workers," just like the company president and the branch manager. There are no bosses at Kinko's.

✗ Reward the team with a special event: pizza for everybody . . . or a catered picnic lunch.

> At Galyan's Trading Company, a huge, hands-on sporting goods store in Columbus, Ohio, an employee told me, "I love working here. They take care of us. If it's real busy, they put food out in the back room for us."

✗ Sponsor a relationship with a needy child or family and give the crew responsibility for the project.

✗ Most communities now have a "Sponsor a Highway" program where businesses take responsibility for keeping a stretch of highway clean and free of litter. It's a good public relations move and is especially popular with Generation X workers, who often have a special concern about environmental issues. It is also a good way to get them involved in a project that helps them see they *can* make a difference.

> One manager at a branch bank asked a local bakery to frost and decorate hamburger buns. For a surprise Friday morning celebration, she posted a banner that read, "You've worked your buns off this week."

✗ Poker is popular with many members of Generation X. Check it out with your staff and consider hosting a poker night.

✗ If you have an employee with a recurring behavior problem and you have spoken to him or her three times and documented your discussions, fire the person. Nothing is worse for morale—yours included—than a complete lack of discipline.

✗ When something bad happens to someone on the staff—like an accident or a death in the family—talk about it. Encourage the whole team to send a card. Teams can become more cohesive during adversity.

✗ Be a coach and people-developer. Be your employees' greatest supporter!

From an Xpert

The Little Things Count
BY JILL EGGLETON BRETT

The twentysomethings of the nineties, myself included, tend to get lost in the shuffle at times—the shuffle being life in general. We are trying to make our way in the world and earn the respect of adults. One way to ease the burden is to reward us with small gestures for a job well done. Remember: the little things count. Showing employees that you care by setting out food in the back room on a busy day says a lot. This gesture not only shows us our efforts are recognized and will be rewarded, but also that you care about us as human beings.

I like the suggestion of keeping up with twentysomething trends. It not only keeps you young, but helps close the generation gap. If we see you wearing the newest beaded necklace or hip necktie, you become more approachable and on our level. We do not want to go to work and be told what to do by someone who looks like our parents. It's a big turn-off. Instead, we appreciate managers who attempt to relate to us instead of writing us off. It fosters a team atmosphere.

Jill Eggleton Brett, 24, is a freelance writer. She has held jobs as a waitress and bartender—and aspires to be a screenwriter. She lives in Cincinnati.

Why Twentysomething Employees Leave

- Limited career growth

- Lack of promotion

- Lack of regular feedback on work performance

- Low pay

- Poor treatment from managers

- Lack of recognition

- Stress, especially stress caused by understaffing

CHAPTER FOUR

Conclusion pg. 83

g

*E*arlier, we talked about how financially savvy twentysomething people can be. Many actually think of *themselves* as marketable commodities—as walking resumes. They know they're needed on the job market—at least in the service industry. They know what the people across the street are paying compared to what their friends are getting across town.

They want to become more marketable by learning new skills and developing expertise in specialized areas. They want feedback to let them know how they're doing and to provide them with guidance about potential growth areas.

How are you at giving feedback? Comfortable enough that you confront a problem immediately? Adept enough that the employee understands the specific improvement you're requesting? Polished enough that you are generally able to avoid making people defensive? These skills are absolutely necessary when it comes to managing Generation X.

✗ Take a seminar or get coaching if you're less than confident about your feedback skills. Employee development requires clear, specific, forthright feedback.

✗ Develop your skills at giving feedback "on the fly." Many times, you will have only a few seconds to say what needs to be said. Give clear, laser-like feedback and direction.

✗ Be a resource about educational opportunities—local community colleges, adult education programs, free universities.

✗ Institute a mentorship program.

> To enrich the working lives of employees at Promus Hotels, job sharing and job swapping are encouraged. Half the candidates for the management program are found within the organization—now more than ever before.

✗ Educate your people about your business. Everyone should know what the goals are, how they'll be measured, where the business is this year compared to last.

✗ When you give staff assignments, include benefits; answer the question, "What's in it for me?" For example, "By preparing these invoices, you will learn a little about our major accounts and how many of our services they use each month." Or, "By calling these customers and telling them about our new fall line, you'll gain experience in public relations."

> Recruiters at the Air Force Academy have learned it's important to make expectations very clear with Generation X. In previous years, the Academy assumed all cadets were committed to "give it a try" for at least three months. They've learned that 30 days is a more realistic expectation these days; they now create a verbal contract that includes "what we'll give you" and "what we require in return."

✗ Encourage employees to teach each other how to do their jobs.

✗ Create a resource center (even a corner in the back room) with a VCR and personal-development videos.

> Production and service training at Fazoli's Italian restaurants is available to all employees in each store on an interactive computer.

✗ Don't expect your employees to change the way they see the world; *do* expect them to learn and grow.

> At Marie Callendar's restaurants and pie shops, managers are trained to be coaches. They are asked to work one-on-one on an ongoing basis with each of their direct reports. Through discussion and roleplaying, they pinpoint specific ways an individual can improve communication and performance.

✗ When you hold training programs, make sure the trainer creates links that help people apply skills to their personal lives along with their jobs. For example, if your staff members are learning better communication skills, show them how these are useful with their families or their young children.

> Sodexho, a worldwide contract food-service business, found that computer-speak—bits and bytes, RAM and ROM—was compounding the generation gap in their organization. They are teaching everyone basic computer skills and language so people are "singing off the same songsheet."

✗ Send your people to seminars and workshops. Can't afford it? Pay for half. Can't afford that? Let them attend on company time. Can't even do that? Pay for parking.

The Tattered Cover, Denver's internationally acclaimed bookstore, begins training people in the reality of work even before they begin the application process. When prospective employees come in to apply for jobs, they are given a letter thanking them for their interest and giving them some basic information about what it's like to work at the Tattered Cover.

"The work is customer-oriented, very detailed, and sometimes physically demanding. Most of us spend long hours on our feet. Dust and printer's ink are part of our daily environment, and applicants must have an adaptable nature because job descriptions here are often loosely defined. We must be flexible enough to fulfill a variety of functions, depending upon what needs are most pressing at any given time."

The letter goes on to explain the benefits and to encourage people to fill out the application—after carefully considering what they've read.

✗ Bring in a trainer for a brown-bag lunch presentation.

A Florida retailer pays half the tuition bill if employees will commit to work at least 20 hours a week until they get their diplomas.

✗ Take an employee or two with you to district meetings and corporate gatherings.

At Kingston Plantation, one of the largest Radisson resorts in the country, all 550 employees are eligible to take part in the Quality Leadership Development (QLD) series. The series includes segments on interviewing and hiring, termination procedures, sexual harassment, worker's compensation, business etiquette, time management, productivity, interpreting the profit and loss statement, and payroll procedures.

Training manager Karen O'Brien Butterworth says, "Here at Kingston, we believe that one of the greatest motivational tools for employees is to enable them to see potential for advancement. We like to introduce them to all the possibilities from the moment they begin their career with us."

Even new hires without aspirations for management appreciate knowing more about the business—and business in general—and say the series has made them feel more involved. The company has found it's grooming more and more young front-line employees for management, and the QLD series has helped them in this effort. Those who complete 150 hours of classes wear a cap and gown at a formal graduation ceremony held at an all-employee celebration.

✗ Supply computer programs that help people manage their money.

✗ Ask each of your people to develop a career map with your assistance.

At the Xpresso Drive-Thru Cafe, where I stop for a latte on days I'm working in my office, one of the Gen X employees posts a question on the blackboard each day. (Which bodily organ do frogs breathe through? What is the oldest board game? Who created the character of Frankenstein?) (Oh, all right. Their skin. Go. Mary Shelley.) Customers who give the correct answer get a double punch on their frequent-coffee-buyer cards, and the employees—all twentysomethings—get to be the "keepers of the answers." I imagine they learn something new with each question and that the topics have provoked some rich conversation.

✗ Watch for opportunities to move people into positions where they can learn new skills.

✗ Create a partnership with a credit union or finance company. Ask its people to come in and teach and advise your staff on money matters.

✗ Don't delegate a task to someone if you're truly certain he or she is not capable of completing it successfully. Find another project where that employee can make a meaningful contribution.

✗ Keep trade magazines on hand; encourage everyone to read and discuss them.

✗ Pass on books you've read. Have a lending library. Draw out a quiet staff member with something chosen especially for him or her: "I understand you're interested in negotiation skills. You might enjoy this book."

Associates III, a high-end interior design firm in Denver, budgets a certain amount of funds each year to encourage employees' community service efforts. For example, the company pays entry fees if an associate wants to participate in the Run for the Cure, the national competition that raises money for breast cancer research and treatment.

Tom Budinick owns a handful of Auntie Anne's soft pretzel outlets in the Midwest. "In wealthy suburbs, the kids don't need to work. Unless it's a satisfying environment, they won't stick around," he says. Tom's employees told him what they wanted most was recognition and feedback—knowing where they stand. So, Tom's employees—even part-timers earning minimum wage—get performance reviews every three months. Small raises are a possibility at each review. To cover the added cost, Tom raised the price of a pretzel 10 cents—with no major complaints from his customers.

Chick-fil-A is strongly committed to steady support of employees. In the past 25 years, the company has awarded $1,000 scholarships to more than 6,000 crew members who have worked an average of 20 hours per week for at least two years. Employees can also qualify for a four-year, $10,000 scholarship through WinShape—"shaping winners"—which exemplifies founder Truett Cathy's commitment to "enabling young people to reach their full potential."

Job sharing and job swapping are popular with twenty-something employees. Occasionally shifting jobs helps people learn more about the company, develop their skills, and get a different perspective. Sheila Wardell, a sales associate at Lands' End in Wisconsin, works one day a week in the returns department. "It lends variety to the job," she says. "I get to learn about another part of the company. Now I understand why people in the returns department actually need all that information they request on the return slips."

From an pert

Challenge Us
BY DANIEL A. CLARK

My parents and my friends' parents have been working for the same companies for 25 years. But here I am, three years out of graduate school, and I'm about to switch to a very different job. I've been teaching college English, but now I'm moving into technical and promotional writing.

Members of Generation X know we are going to hold many different jobs in our lives; we want to pick up skills and experience that can be woven into a "career." We want three years of experience, not one year of experience three times.

Don't be surprised if your efforts to develop us aren't met with overwhelming gratitude. We've learned the hard way that there's no such thing as "employer loyalty"— and "employee loyalty" is just youthful naivete. That's not to say you shouldn't invest in us; if the effort to develop us is honest and will actually lead to new responsibility, respect, and experience, you'll get a lot for the effort.

A big paycheck isn't going to be enough when the job offers no new challenges. We've seen our parents' generation settle for and lose interest in safe, secure—but dull— occupations. We don't want those jobs, and our reluctance to buy into that part of the "American Dream" is why we have been misunderstood as slackers. We want to work; we never had the illusion we wouldn't have to. But we want to be challenged by our work. We want to use our creativity. We want to change and grow.

Daniel A. Clark, 26, teaches English. He is planning on getting out of academia—"the frustrations are too great"—and into editing and publishing—"probably equally frustrating, but with better career potential." Daniel lives in Cincinnati.

How to Handle a Recurring Employee Issue

1. Identify the problem and explain how it affects the organization.

   When people repeatedly don't show up on time other employees have to handle set-up, and morale suffers.

   When we don't handle customer complaints efficiently, we lose their business.

2. Give one, two, or three concrete examples of the behavior.

   You were 20 minutes late last Wednesday; yesterday you came back from your break 15 minutes late; now, this morning, it's 9:30 and the schedule says you were due at 9:00.

   You put Mr. Brown on hold this morning and never got back to him; yesterday your phone rang 10 times before you answered.

3. Request that the behavior change.

   This needs to change.

   Please give customers top priority.

4. Implement an action plan with a timeline and observable behavior.

   I'm asking that you be here on time—or even a few minutes early— every day for the next two weeks.

   Let's agree that you will answer all calls by the fourth ring and leave customers holding no longer than 45 seconds.

5. Follow up.

   Let's get together two weeks from today—February 15 at 10:00 to check your record.

   Let's check in with each other two weeks from today—that will be September 30—to see how it's going. How's 3:00?

CHAPTER FIVE

INVOLVE US

Your people are much more likely to do a good job when they feel their opinions are valued. When they're involved in a decision, they have ownership in it. Your bottom-line results will increase dramatically when your front-line people feel they "own" the business. United Airlines seems to have taken off—literally and figuratively—since it was purchased by its employees.

✗ Pull the whole staff together and encourage them to create a "big, hairy, audacious goal." Make it measurable. Set a deadline. Post it where it's highly visible to the staff. Celebrate with everyone when they reach the goal.

✗ Take time to work side-by-side with each staff member, letting him or her know you want to learn innovative practices from them. Solicit suggestions about how to improve processes.

✗ Give an award for an innovative idea.

✗ Put up pictures of everybody on the staff.

✗ Let the whole staff choose the Employee of the Month.

✗ Take an employee on a customer call.

✗ When outsiders visit your store, department, or plant, ask employees to give them a tour and explain the business.

At the Broadmoor Hotel in Colorado Springs, once the goals for the year are established, each department meets to outline its specific contribution. Then each manager meets with line employees to ask for their commitment to contribute to the department's goals. By involving everyone in goal setting, each employee understands how he or she affects the success of the business.

At one Marie Callendar's restaurant and pie shop, the general manager, Jody, always ran the daily preshift meeting. The regular format for the preshift meeting is provided on a form, and the manager collects the appropriate information for each day's meeting. When Jody came in one day with laryngitis, she asked one of the employees to lead the meeting. This small gesture made the employee feel more involved. Now all preshift meetings are led by employees.

At the AlphaGraphics print shop in Wilmington, North Carolina, the whole staff gets involved in an annual planning meeting. The store closes on a Saturday afternoon. After everyone is served lunch, the staff revisits its mission statement: Does it still work? Does anything need to be changed? Then everyone gets involved in a S.W.O.T. analysis, evaluating the store's strengths, weaknesses, opportunities, threats. The owners find that when the staff members analyze their own performance, they're tougher on themselves than anyone else would be. People are assigned tasks and owner Dick Stone uses the ideas to write his annual business plan. Then, before the game on Super Bowl Sunday, Dick presents highlights and an overview of the plan.

✗ Explain the monthly spreadsheet to everyone and help them understand their contribution to it.

✗ When you get employee input at a staff meeting, let them know the truth: that you will consider their input, but *may* make another decision. *Do* get back to them to let them know how you used their input and how you made your final decision.

✗ Take the mystery out of decision-making; let your staff know how decisions are made in your organization.

A resort hotel in San Diego keeps a "rumors" bulletin board in the employee meeting room. When employees hear rumors, they jot them down and post them. At regular staff meetings, managers read the rumors aloud and respond to them so that everyone has "the scoop."

✗ Take an employee or two with you to a seminar or conference; encourage them to speak up about their experiences on the job.

✗ When the annual report is released, get everybody a copy or give them a printed summary. Choose two or three important points to discuss in a staff meeting.

> Due to a lack of affordable housing, the high cost of living, and the shrinking labor pool, virtually all ski areas are struggling to find enough help. To get current employees involved in solving the problem, Winter Park Resort in Colorado rewards those who recruit friends. When the recruit stays through the whole season, the referring friend receives $50. Last year 60 employees walked away with a little extra cash.

✗ Choose an employee you trust and ask for feedback on how you're doing as a coach and supporter.

> Boston Chicken has installed sophisticated information-gathering technology in its stores that allows employees to evaluate their workday. Some of the questions ask, "Do you feel you are properly trained? Do you feel you are selling quality products? Are you giving good service?" By encouraging employees to input a quick evaluation at the end of each day, operators are able to keep track of employee satisfaction and take preventive measures to reduce turnover.

Pete Harman's company owns more than 250 KFC stores. To attract and retain managers, he has instituted a program that allows his managers to own as much as 30% of the stores where they work. The company helps them buy the stock and guarantees the loan. The result is a management turnover rate of 12%, which is astoundingly low for the quick-service industry.

Within hours of the Oklahoma City bombing, employees at the Doubletree hotels in Tulsa, Oklahoma, mounted a local relief effort to support the victims of the tragedy. The initiative quickly grew into a chainwide campaign involving 16,000 employees nationwide and produced a $28,000 contribution. Doubletree donated thousands of its trade-marked chocolate chip cookies to rescue workers and families of victims.

It all began with a creative idea for involving employees in a fund drive to benefit the bombing victims. On April 21 and 28, for a $3 donation, employees in Tulsa could come to work in casual clothes instead of their uniforms. When the corporate office learned of the plan, they gave immediate support by sending out a fax to their 109 hotels nationwide, encouraging similar efforts. Doubletree hotels across the country responded in a variety of ways, some that involved guests in fundraising.

✗ Get someone on your staff to conduct exit interviews. When employees quit, follow up a few weeks later to learn all you can from them about your work environment and management practices. Employees who leave are a rich source of valuable information and feedback.

Outstanding entrepreneurial twentysomethings have a unique opportunity to run their own business at Chick-fil-A. Whereas most fast-food franchises require a major investment—usually upwards of $200,000—Chick-fil-A operators make a financial commitment of only $5,000. All operators are guaranteed a base annual income of $30,000 along with a 50/50 split of net profits, after paying the company 15% of gross sales.

From an pert

Using Staff Meetings To Increase Involvement
BY MARJORIE J. MILNOR

When I worked as a lifeguard at a state university recreation center, the aquatics director made sure everyone was involved from day one.

Staff meetings were held four times a semester. During the meeting, the director discussed the important points, and printed others in a "take-home agenda," leaving time for discussion. The last agenda item was always "Staff Time." Comments were to be brief, and each staff member could bring up anything. Comments varied from new staff saying hello to more experienced staff to addressing problems with systems and equipment. Either the director or the appropriate crew chief would address those concerns at the meeting or note the problem and look into it.

After the meeting, all attendees filled out evaluation forms, addressing questions like, "Did the meeting educate and involve everyone?"; "Was the meeting appropriate?"; and "What new thing did you learn at the meeting?" The final question was open-ended, asking for suggestions. These were then evaluated and acted upon by the director and the crew chiefs.

Everyone felt there was room for their comments before, during, and after meetings. Everyone was informed and able to handle questions from other lifeguards and the public. Communication lines were open; feedback was swift and clear. This meant a smoothly running operation, without the rumors, misunderstandings; and frustration that come from a lack of involvement.

Marjorie Milnor is a freelance writer, editor, and word processor. She is 24. She lives in New York.

How To Deal With a Recurring Employee Issue That You've Already Handled and Documented Three Times

1. At the end of Round Two, inform the employee that one more recurrence will result in termination.

   This is the second time we have discussed this and you have agreed to change your behavior. I've made notes both times in my files. If this occurs again, I will have to ask you to leave.

2. Fire 'em.

   Many GOOD employees leave because they don't see recurring labor problems HANDLED by their managers. Do the right thing.

CHAPTER SIX

LIGHTEN UP

I recently talked to a company president who is in his fifties. I knew his oldest son had graduated from college in the spring, and I asked him how his son was doing. "Well," he grumbled, "he got a great job with a prestigious insurance company. But he quit this month. When I asked him why he quit, he said the job wasn't fun. What I want to know is: what does *that* have to do with work?"

It has a lot to do with work these days. Generation Xers grew up in pretty serious times. They're looking for some fun—and they say it's a priority for them on the job.

Most of us managers have taken life pretty seriously; that's how we got where we are. Sometimes our work lives are so busy that we get focused on the details—and treat them as if they were life or death matters. If you're managing the emergency room, this is an appropriate attitude. If not, remind yourself regularly that, sure, your work is important—very important—but that life will probably continue pretty much as we know it, even if the details at work aren't quite the way you wanted.

101

You don't need to be the Vice-President in Charge of Fun yourself, but you can urge others to take on that role. Encourage fun and enjoyment, including light competition, while the work gets done.

> Woodward Governor, a manufacturer in Fort Collins, Colorado, is located in a beautiful setting with acres of grass and lovely landscaping. The grounds crews hold light competitions: one crew mows diagonally while the other mows horizontally; they time themselves to see who is fastest.

✗ Fill an employee's workstation with balloons.

✗ Post cartoons that take a humorous look at issues facing you and your staff.

✗ Let employees choose music to work by. If customers are affected, the decision will, of course, need to take them into account.

✗ Hire a juggler for the lunch hour. Teach everybody to juggle.

✗ During lean times, go ahead with the annual picnic or the softball league. They're even *more* important when times are rough.

> During a particularly low sales period, the manager of a demoralized telemarketing team asked everybody to work *under* their desks for an hour. The energy changed and the team met its goal for the day.

✗ Appoint a Company Mom on a rotating basis. The Mom is in charge of a small amount of petty cash and morale for the week.

✗ Show old movies at lunch in the cafeteria; you can't go wrong with The Three Stooges or Laurel and Hardy.

At TEXTRON Turbine Engine Components, two computers are reserved for education. The computers are loaded with video games. At lunchtime, they are used by a group of employees who are zealously involved in an ongoing golf tournament.

✗ Give everybody a pair of Groucho Marx glasses with nose and moustache.

✗ Ask everybody to wear their favorite baseball hats . . . or their favorite band T-shirts . . . or their wildest slacks.

At Macaroni Grill, a chain of trendy Italian restaurants, waiters and waitresses write their names upside down with a crayon on the paper tablecloth when they introduce themselves.

✗ Allow a certain amount of socializing. It's healthy.

Tension had been building for a couple of weeks at a computer access company. Everybody was on the verge of losing it. A punching clown arrived in the back room. It relieved the stress and reminded people, "This isn't brain surgery."

✗ Have a dress-down day.

The corporate offices of Wendy's International in Dublin, Ohio, have "summer hours." Each employee is assigned to one of three teams. Each team is assigned two afternoons off each month in the summer.

At a Speidel TEXTRON watch-manufacturing plant, a trumpet call is broadcast on the PA system and everyone does a set of light exercises. They're a little zany . . . and they're great stress relievers.

At an NCR plant in South Carolina, the song "Heard it Through the Grapevine" is broadcast throughout the plant two or three times a month, signaling everybody to get out their juggling cubes for a jugglerama.

Planned Parenthood invites new mothers to bring infants to work with them until they reach the toddler stage.

ARC International, a Denver-based consulting company, held an Ugly T-Shirt contest at an annual meeting that brought the Japanese and American components of the business together. It was a great cross-cultural team builder.

Last year, at a direct marketing company, managers in one department let everyone off one hour early on March 4 (Get it? March forth!). Employees left to the tune of a kazoo band of managers playing "Stars and Stripes Forever."

✗ Eliminate unnecessary stress. Too much emphasis on crisis management causes twentysomething workers to look for other jobs.

> Everyone at Wilson Learning Corporation gets a Mickey Mouse watch after three months on the job.

✗ For a quick tension reliever, hold a Nerf basketball game.

> A firefighter with the City of Westminster, Colorado, says he is considering becoming a management consultant. "I know what a fire is," he says, "I've been putting them out for 20 years. I constantly see managers burning up over things that, in my estimation, aren't even smoking."

From an Xpert

Benefits of a Friendly Work Atmosphere
BY PAMELA MCINNIS

"Lighten up" is about the best advice managers of twentysomething workers can heed.

Somewhere along the way, the dream of this generation shifted. Some say it was in response to the economy and what we could realistically attain; others attribute the change to our parents' dissatisfaction. Whatever the reason, most of us aren't dreaming about homes with picket fences, two-car garages, and 1.5 kids. We subscribe to the "you only live once so enjoy it while it lasts" philosophy. Since most of us are at work at least 40 hours a week, this means we must enjoy being there. We're not lazy. On the contrary, if we like what we do for a living and feel at home where we do it, most of us will give 110%. Burning the midnight oil to complete a project is something we'll do gladly as long as we're in good company.

In my first job out of college, I was an administrative assistant. The first three months, my supervisor dictated orders, gave stern lectures, and glared at me through his glasses. I worked hard, but I couldn't get into my projects. I love to write, but when asked to compile something—a simple PR piece, seminar materials, or assessment reports—my work was stiff and lifeless.

At some point, this supervisor began to change. He told jokes, discussed movies, and offered criticism in a gentler manner. He had his staff over for a cookout, and went out for coffee with us after work once in a while "just to talk." My uneasiness at work faded. My creativity skyrocketed. The work I submitted was almost always exactly what he needed. I didn't rush out of work at 5:00 P.M. anxious for a breath of fresh air. With nothing more than a friendlier, more team-oriented atmosphere, the quality of work improved, and all of us—the boss included—enjoyed our jobs more.

Pamela McInnis, 25, recently left her job as a college career counselor to begin working on a masters' degree. She aspires to be a successful author of short fiction and professor of English. Pamela lives in Baltimore, Maryland.

"Managers need to understand that twentysomethings are a different generation. Most managers don't realize that. They don't realize that it takes a different style. They need to be taught that this is a new generation quite different from where they were at that age."

—Fast Food Worker, Age 18

The Manager from Hell

. . . thinks employees must "pay their dues" before they can be respected, listened to, or praised.

. . . thinks a paycheck is all the "thanks" an employee should need.

. . . institutes a new policy or procedure every time someone does something less than perfectly.

. . . models the "my way or the highway" style of management.

. . . begins sentences with, "When I was your age. . . ."

. . . mixes frustrations from personal life with work situations.

. . . isn't willing to learn, change, and grow.

CHAPTER SEVEN

WALK YOUR TALK

Sometimes we forget what an impact we have. Employees tell me they watch to see how their boss closes the car door when arriving in the morning; it's their cue for what kind of a day it's going to be. Others tell me the manager is the "weather setter," that, if he or she is gloomy, it's likely to be a stormy day for everyone; if the manager is upbeat, it's likely to be clear and sunny.

One of the X Generation's complaints about managers is that we don't practice what we preach—we give lip service to things like positive attitude, empowerment, employee involvement, valuing our people. But we often don't back up our words with the appropriate actions.

In New York, a manager went to lunch across the street from the retail store where she was to begin work that afternoon. Unbeknownst to her—or to them—three of her soon-to-be employees were having lunch. Everyone in the restaurant that day noticed how rude she was to the waiter. You can be certain she had a tough time establishing credibility with those employees!

CEO Tom Chappell says, "The greatest vulnerability for Tom's of Maine is if it doesn't walk its talk. If we are putting promises out there that we can't live up to internally, then we're just setting ourselves up to be hurt. The media will expose that. We have to be very careful that we're living up to the promises we're making."

Your people are ruthless observers. When you tell them you value respect, they want to know if you honestly do, and they may test you.

Employees who are treated poorly turn right around and treat customers as they are treated. You are a role model for your people.

✗ Model the attitude and behavior you want from them.

✗ Welcome your staff members with a smile, thank them, and get to know them as people. They will translate your actions into their jobs—welcoming guests and customers, thanking them, and encouraging them to come again.

A few years ago at the Plaza Hotel in New York City, every room in the hotel was to turn over within three hours. Every manager—from executives to front-line supervisors—was assigned to a team that would strip beds or clean bathrooms or vacuum carpets. The housekeeping staff was the quality assurance team that day, making sure the work was done with excellence.

✗ Think of your staff members as customers; treat them with the quality of respect you give a key customer.

✗ Take time to step into all the job roles in your department occasionally.

Lee Cockerell is executive vice president of resorts at Walt Disney World. "The world from the window of my office looks pretty good," says Lee. "So, if I want to know what's really going on, I have to roll up my sleeves and get involved." Lee goes to work in operations two to three times per month, cooking burgers and fries—and taking tickets for the haunted house. Once or twice per week, he holds meetings with 15 hourly employees. Someone with a laptop computer takes notes, and Lee meets with the same group 90 days later to follow up. The meetings allow him to speak personally with seven or eight hundred cast members per year. Lee also teaches a leadership class to front-line managers, who are surprised to find an executive rather than a trainer as their instructor. His objective: to set the example.

✗ Don't "pass the buck" by telling your staff members they have to do something because "the District Manager said so," or "they dreamed it up at corporate." Discuss new policies that come from above with the appropriate people until you feel you can honestly stand behind them.

✗ If you're having a rough day, let your people know, but keep it general. They don't need to know all the gory details. Have a colleague available—by phone, if necessary—to act as your sounding board.

✗ Create an environment in which it is acceptable to make mistakes—and learn from them. Share examples of your own mistakes and how they helped you grow.

Last year, foremen at the Winter Park Resort in Colorado announced to the ski-lift operators they would evaluate their supervisors at the end of the season. All totaled, supervisors earned an A average!

✗ Make your own growth visible to your staff. When you agree to make an improvement, post it. Being a leader today is a public event.

✗ Be willing to admit when you've made a mistake. Acknowledge it and apologize.

Sean Conley, regional director of guest services for Marie Callender's, stopped by the Marie Callender's restaurant near his home recently to pick up some papers. It was obvious that the staff was deluged with business and that there weren't enough employees on hand to offer the efficient and friendly service guests expect. Sean grabbed an apron, picked up a station, and waited four tables. "Call me whenever you need me," Sean told the staff. "It's my neighborhood and I'm glad to help."

Everyone at Walt Disney World wears a nametag with his or her first name and the city and state or country of birth. No titles are included, even for executives. The place of birth is a great conversation-starter with guests and other cast members.

✗ Listen fully. Everyone wants to be heard.

✗ Have a "monthly check-up." Ask for and genuinely accept feedback on a regular basis.

✗ Dress down occasionally; show staff you're human.

After the childcare provider called in sick, Dick Fleming, president of the Denver Chamber of Commerce, gave a speech with his six-month-old perched on one hip.

✗ If your company still has an executive bathroom, lunchroom, or parking space, get rid of it!

✗ Show up at extracurricular events. Financial support is not enough; it's your presence that really matters.

✗ Tell an occasional joke on yourself.

✗ Take this quick test: 1. Jot down a brief list of the qualities you want in your employees. 2. Give yourself a grade that evaluates *your* performance on each item on the list.

✗ Honor your commitments. Do what you say you're going to do.

At the AlphaGraphics print shop in Littleton, Colorado, most "re-dos" are caused by the pressman, and the manager fills out a form detailing the error. One day recently when a problem occurred, the pressman came to store manager Tammy Bradish and asked, "What did I do this time?" Tammy responded that she herself had caused the problem—and asked the pressman if *he* would like to fill out the form. He was pleased to oblige.

Manage Us by Example
BY CHRISTOPHER CARBONI

"Do as I say, not as I do" was the favorite saying of a manager I once had. He watched the clock and docked anyone who was not ready and hard at work the precise moment the shift began. Yet he frequently took two- and three-hour lunches. He rarely was found in his office and more often could be found in the cafeteria having a cigarette—something we were not even allowed to clock out to do.

As you can imagine, no one wanted to work for him. And it showed. The monthly goal was usually around $1.4 million. I don't think we did better than about $850,000 during any of the three months he was the manager.

In my book, the way to manage is by example. What you do—not what you say—speaks loudest. Intimidation is for hypocrites.

Christopher Carboni, 28, owns his own advertising, design, and publishing business. He says he sometimes struggles with the question of whether to hire employees in his own age group or to seek more experienced help. He lives in West Seneca, New York.

X

"I have a basic inability to work a job that doesn't make sense to me."

—Jennet Hunt, Graduate Student, Age 26

Meaningful Rewards

- Cash

- Personal freedom (a day off, for example)

- Opportunities for development

- Praise

A JUST REWARD

*I*f you've read this far, you deserve something for yourself. Being a manager today is a daunting and demanding role.

I believe your employees will come to you years later and thank you for the way you touched their lives. But I know there are days—sometimes weeks—when none of your people are even pleasant to you—let alone grateful!

So, for all the things you do that are extraordinary, and as a special reward for traveling all the way to the end of this book, I leave you with a few strategies for giving yourself the pat on the back you so richly deserve.

✗ Send yourself a bouquet of fresh flowers.

✗ Take yourself to a baseball game.

✗ Take five minutes off. Close the door. Think of all the things you've done well in the last week.

✗ Go fishing.

✗ Get a massage.

✗ Go to a seminar on something that has nothing to do with your job—just something interesting you'd like to know a little more about.

✗ Buy yourself a greeting card that says something you want to hear. Put it in a place where you will see it regularly.

✗ Give yourself an afternoon to be absolutely purposeless.

✗ Get your car washed.

✗ Send the kids to day care and take the day to be at home totally by yourself.

✗ Go to a matinee.

✗ Shoot pool.

✗ Get a pedicure.

✗ Buy yourself a journal. Keep a record of your successes.

✗ Find a colleague who will agree to do something outrageous with you to celebrate a success. For example, if you reach your sales goal this month, the two of you will hit 20 buckets of balls at the driving range.

✗ Buy a bottle of champagne. Before dinner, host a toast in your honor!

True-False Test

1. Members of Generation X tend to be materialistic.	T	F
2. Most of today's young workers are whiners.	T	F
3. Twentysomethings are impatient.	T	F
4. Xers have a "you owe me" attitude.	T	F
5. They are not willing to work hard.	T	F

Answers:

1. **F**—The majority are having a hard time making ends meet. They will inherit an overwhelming public debt. They worry they will not have enough money to pay for a home and their own children's education. Many were responsible for significant amounts of money when they were children; therefore, they are financially literate and fiscally rather conservative. They want to get out of debt. They know what others are paying—and they will "shop" for the best salaries and benefits. But they are not materialistic—material wealth and status items are often scorned upon by this generation.

2. **F**—This generation faces some rather daunting challenges—declining wages, increased job competition, and skyrocketing healthcare costs, for example—yet most are philosophical about the problems they're inheriting.

3. **T**—Most of them probably are. Weren't you when you first got started? It's part of being twentysomething, always has been.

4. **F**—No more so than any other generation. We have a serious problem in American business with entitlement—the "you owe me" attitude. But Generation X is no more guilty of this than the rest of us.

5. **F**—Most twentysomethings are willing to work very hard. Generally speaking, though, they do not want to be taken advantage of; for example, if they are contracted for a 40-hour work week, they believe it's unfair for us to expect them to give 50 on a regular basis. We may need to rethink what it means "to work hard."

About the Author

CLAIRE RAINES is considered the nation's leading expert on Generation X—who they are, what makes them different, and how to develop successful ways of working with them. She is a dynamic speaker, award-winning author, and highly regarded organizational consultant.

Ms. Raines is the coauthor of *Twentysomething: Managing and Motivating Today's New Work Force,* named one of the thirty best business books of 1992. She has been featured widely in the media, including *USA Today, Training Magazine, Working Woman,* and *Personnel Journal.*

In her consulting practice, Ms. Raines works with companies to provide the tools for understanding young workers. In order to create an environment that supports and develops them, she designs management systems based on Generation X values.

As an internationally recognized speaker, Ms. Raines has received rave reviews for her keynote speeches, which help audiences better understand the generations. Her presentations offer thought-provoking facts, engaging anecdotes, and practical applications. Claire Raines's clients include MasterCard, McDonald's, Sprint, T.G.I. Friday's, Wendy's International, Lincoln Electric, Holiday Inn Worldwide, and Brinker International. For availability and fee information, call Jaclyn Yelich, (303) 399-0630.